D1297354

THE AMERICAN INDIAN IN FILM

by

Michael Hilger

The Scarecrow Press, Inc.
Metuchen, N.J., & London
1986

Library of Congress Cataloging-in-Publication Data

Hilger, Michael, 1940–
    The American Indian in film.

    Bibliography: p.
    Includes indexes.
    1. Indians in motion pictures. I. Title.
PN1995.9.I48H54   1986   791.43'09'093520397   86-10061
ISBN 0-8108-1905-8

Copyright © 1986 by Michael Hilger
Manufactured in the United States of America

To

my Mother, Marion,

and

the memory of my Father, Donatus

ACKNOWLEDGMENTS

Thanks to Veda Stone, who got me started on this project; to Steve Swords and Marek Labinsky, who helped me with the research; to Nick Hilger and John Hoogesteger, who taught me about the problems of urban Indians; to Jan Kippenhan and Sharon Duerkop, who typed the manuscript; and to Melinda Smith, with appreciation for her encouragement, help, and companionship.

CONTENTS

A NOTE ON FORMAT

The films are arranged chronologically to illustrate the de-
velopment and sometimes strange mixture of images and themes
in the historical periods. The principle of selection is that
the American Indian be a significant part of the film, in terms
of either character or plot. For each film, the title, releasing
company, date and director is followed by a brief plot sum-
mary based on information from periodicals, reference books,
and viewing. The focus in the summaries is on the actions of
the Indian characters, with their names and those of the actors who play them when available; whites are referred to as
the "hero/heroine" or "villain" unless the character is a historical figure associated with Indians, such as George Custer
or William Cody, and often major parts of the plots relevant
to the white characters are omitted. Where appropriate, comments from contemporary film reviews on the Indian characters
are added to the summaries. The introductions to each period
use representative films to show in some detail, and with reference to film techniques, how individual films reflect the context of the period.

References to film reviews are parenthetical in the text,
and the year of the review is the same as that of the film unless otherwise noted. The Variety reviews are taken from the
Variety Film Reviews published by Garland Press and the
references to them include the day and the month, the main
headings in the individual volumes which are arranged by
year. References to all other newspapers and magazines are
to the individual issues.

INTRODUCTION: THE FICTIONAL INDIAN

An incident from John Ford's <u>Cheyenne Autumn</u> dramatizes
the two prevailing images of the American Indian in film. A
newspaper editor rushes into the newsroom reading out loud
the typical headlines, "Bloodthirsty Savages Rape and Pillage"
and then notes that such an approach is just not news any-
more, they should now "grieve for the noble red man"--and
thus sell more newspapers. Like the editor, filmmakers from
the silents to the present have used the images of the bloodthirsty savage and the noble but doomed savage as fictions
to emphasize the superiority of their white heroes, to comment on contemporary political issues or to serve the needs
of the western genre. As the summaries of the films in each
historical period will show, even such great directors as D.W.
Griffith and John Ford portray the Indian as always too good
or too bad; as such they are often the most extreme fictions
in the western, a genre which seldom comes very close to
reality.[1]

   In narrative film, the American Indian is usually a sym-
bol, a representation of ideas and values that reflect two
major themes. Associated with the image of the bloodthirsty
savage is the theme of the Indian as enemy of the white's
progress in westward expansion and as adversary used by the
western hero to prove himself. The idea of manifest destiny
of the 1840s suggested that it was God's plan for whites to
explore and settle all parts of the continent. Many filmmakers used these white explorers and settlers to illustrate this
idea by almost always having them triumph over hostile Indians,
usually with the help of the army or an individual hero. In
the western, the male protagonist demonstrates his heroism
by surviving in a hostile landscape made even more dangerous
by the fierce Indian tribes that inhabit it. However, Indians
are not only the worthy enemies of the white hero; they are
also the victims.

   Associated with the image of the noble savage in western

films is the theme that the Indians are doomed because, as
primitive children of nature, they ultimately have no power
to resist manifest destiny and thus will be inevitable victims
of the superior white race. Indians portrayed as children of
nature frequently become objects of paternalism who need to
be helped by heroes since they can be so easily manipulated
by villains, be they outlaws or Indian agents. In fact, the
Indians of the films seem never to be able to recognize villains; they are constantly being incited to go on the warpath
for someone else's evil purposes.

Generally, film-stereotyped Indian men and women have
childlike, primitive emotions: if treated well they are capable
of powerful love, loyalty and gratitude; if treated badly, of
tenacious, fierce vengeance. Their goodness or badness is
always measured by their reaction to whites, never by their
intrinsic nature as American Indians, except in some recent
films. For example, the cinematic Indian woman, usually a
dark, beautiful young maiden or "princess," has a special
ability to recognize the superiority of the white man and will
often fall in love with one rather than with an Indian. Because of her exotic beauty and her willingness to serve, the
Indian maiden is an appealing companion for a white man; for
example, she will often rescue a white man from her own people
and, occasionally, as a wife, will even commit suicide to remove
herself as an obstacle to her husband's desire for a white
woman. In fact, because of the taboo of miscegenation, the
Indian wife of a white man frequently meets her end before
the film is over. The Indian woman who is not a companion
to the white man and who is older is often a "bad" Indian--a
fat, ugly "squaw" who, especially when she is in a group,
delights in the torture of the heroes. The half-breed woman,
often a femme fatale who drives white men to dangerous passion, is a bad Indian, who must die before the end of the film.
However, the typical fictional Indian woman represents the
willingness to serve, protect and be loyal to the white man,
allowing her to be portrayed as a very good, though often
tragic, Indian.

The male Indian screen character is also good if he is
a friend and loyal companion to the white man. The most
well-known Indian characters fit this image: Friday (a Carib
Indian) and Robinson Crusoe; Chingachgook and Hawkeye;
Tonto and the Lone Ranger; Little Beaver and Red Ryder;
and Cochise and Tom Jeffords. In each of these friendships

the white man is dominant, but the two learn from each other and do share a deep affection. Another basis for friendship is education; Indian men educated in white colleges often show their loyalty and affection for whites in addition to using their knowledge to help their tribes. Such young Indian men are also the most appealing to white women, though occasionally romance occurs with a "wild" Indian. The Indian man is almost always attracted to the white woman and often struggles with a desire for the woman and white society despite a sense of responsibility to his tribe. As was true with the mixed romances of the Indian woman, the man's involvement with the white woman almost always leads to rejection or his death at the end of the film. Older Indian men usually have friendships with whites as surrogate fathers, since many plots involve a white man or woman kidnapped or rescued and adopted by the Indians. Such fathers are often kind and wise old chiefs, a character type that is probably the strongest representation of the good Indian male.

The Indian man is portrayed as bad if he is an enemy of whites or a threat to white women. Half-breeds or leaders of hostile Apache bands (like Geronimo) are the Indians most often presented as devious, unscrupulous, and fierce enemies who will use ambush and other guerrilla tactics. Such Indian men are also threats to society because their rebelliousness and vengeance sometimes leads them to rape and kidnap white women. In fact, bands of Indians, often not identified by tribe, constitute the stock evil forces in the western with their ambushes and attacks on farms, forts, cabins, pony express riders, trains, stagecoaches, wagon trains, etc. Such Indians, like the villains of melodramas, are almost always routed by the heroes and finally come across as poor fighters who can be shot like ducks in a shooting gallery.

Although many white Americans may accept these images and the more common stereotypes of Indians as drunken and lazy because of the number of westerns they have seen in the theatres and now on television, they can begin to see the phoniness of the fictional Indian with just a little study of the history and culture of Native Americans. This, in a sense, is the easy part; what is more difficult is to interpret the images and recognize the film techniques that send and reinforce more subtle messages.

From the beginning, filmmakers have repeated and

played upon certain film techniques in their portrayal of Indians, the most notable of which are long shots, camera
angles, placement of characters in the frame, editing, music,
and acting. The long shot, which emphasizes the setting,
often stresses the landscape of the West, with either hostile
Indians hiding and threatening to attack or conquered Indians
vanishing into the horizon in long processions. High angle
shots, in which the audience looks down on the subject, may
suggest the vulnerability of the whites about to be ambushed
by Indians. Low angle shots, in which the audience looks
up at the subject, can emphasize the threat of the Indian
lurking above his victims or the power of the hero whom
the audience consistently sees from a low angle. Composition,
the placement of the characters in the frame, commonly
stresses the superiority of heroes because they are often
higher or more central or more to the foreground of the picture than the Indians. Editing, especially crosscutting between the pursuers and the pursued, can build the suspense
of the inevitable Indian attack on the whites or vice versa;
quick cuts can emphasize individual atrocities or large numbers of Indians falling from their horses, cut down by an
often small group of whites. Music in the form of the bugle
call signals the ultimate rescue by the cavalry, whereas
standard drum rhythms warn the audience that Indians are
threatening. Finally, actors (often whites playing major Indian roles and wearing standard Hollywood costumes) portray
either the woodenly taciturn Indian who speaks with only
slightly more eloquence than Tarzan or the emotional and
fierce Indian who wildly contorts his face and emits other-
worldly war whoops.

    The repetition of these techniques through each histor-
ical period is what really impresses the fictional Indian on the
minds of audiences. Sometimes subtly, often openly, these
film devices send the message that Indians, be they noble or
bloodthirsty, are inferior to whites. Fairly early in the history of film, reviewers, because of their knowledge of film
technique and the plot formulas of westerns, recognized the
fictional Indian, as their comments quoted in the summaries
of the films will indicate. As the body of films grew, the
reviewers were more able to see the evolution of fictional
Indians in larger contexts. The purpose of this book is to
provide the reader with the even larger context of many
silent and most of the sound films that deal with Indians from
the beginning of cinema to the present. With such a context

the reader, like the film reviewers, can begin to interpret the plot and film techniques of individual films and to realize that the fiction of these films reveals little about real American Indians but a lot about the evolution of white American values.

NOTE

1. For the best full-length treatment see O'Connor's The Hollywood Indian and Stedman's Shadows of the Indian. For good shorter studies, see Spears' "The Indian on the Screen," Price's "The Stereotyping of North American Indians in Motion Pictures," Marsden and Nachbar's "Images of Native Americans in Popular Film," and Calder's "Taming the Natives" in There Must Be a Lone Ranger.

THE SILENT FILMS

Filmmakers of the silent era produced many narrative films about American Indians. For instance, among the films of the first star of the westerns, Bronco Billy, are The Cowboy and the Squaw, The Dumb Half-Breed's Defense, An Indian Girl's Love, The Faithful Indian, and The Tribe's Penalty (Weaver 30-31); and among the films produced at the first movie studios in New Jersey are His Indian Bride, How the Boys Fought the Indians, The Indian Land Grab, The Redman and the Child, Red Man's Honor, An Up-to-Date Squaw, and The True Heart of an Indian.[1] Although a significant number of such films are no longer extant, the ones that remain and contemporary film reviews indicate that filmmakers had a generally sympathetic view of the American Indian, especially in the early part of the silent era, which was less than thirty years after the western Indian wars. This sympathy was usually expressed in Indian characters who were noble but wronged or doomed, although the bloodthirsty image became more popular toward the end of the silent era.

Contemporary reviews of the early films indicate the controversy over the sympathetic portrayal of the American Indian. In a 1912 review of the Bison-101 Headliners, a series of westerns, Louis R. Harrison disapproves of the images of Indians as victims in these films and argues that it was historically appropriate for whites, the "representatives of progress," to overcome Indians, the "representatives of degeneration." He characterizes the Indian as a person who used only "that part of his brain which enabled him to be crafty in the hunt for food" and as "a barbarian" more fierce than those of early Europe. On the other hand, the white man "cultivated brain along with brawn" and Harrison believes the American settler was able to conquer the Indians because he was "a man, every inch of him, and the iron in his blood has descended to those who promulgated the Monroe doctrine" (Moving Picture World 27 April 320-322). Harrison's view of the Indian and white settler here and in other reviews represents

not only the themes of white supremacy and manifest destiny,
but also the kind of racial prejudice that demanded the image
of the bloodthirsty savage.

Harrison's need to write such an editorial suggests, however, that the noble, wronged, and disappearing Indian was
a key image in the early films. Another reviewer for Moving
Picture World, writing in 1911, represents this dominant view
of the Indian. He argues that the public is aware that Indians have been "misjudged and slandered in the past" primarily
because of the new moving pictures, which "are helping to set
the red man right in history and in his position before the
American people." The reviewer points out that the best Indian films hold up the nobility of the Indian way of life to the
"belated admiration" of the white audience and concludes that
"this tendency to do the Indian justice runs through all the
pictures" and accounts "for the continued popularity of Indian
films" (5 Aug 271).

Such a concern for the plight of the Indian remains
through much of this period and finds probably its strongest
expression in the Vanishing American (1925). Although this
film is very sympathetic to the American Indian, it uses the
fiction of the noble but doomed savage to stress the superiority of white society and the Christian religion in particular.
At the beginning the filmmakers quote Herbert Spenser's idea
that in history, as in nature, the fittest survive. They then
use a recurring character called Nophaie, the Warrior, to illustrate how the Indian loses the Darwinian battle for survival
to the whites.

In a long prologue depicting the history of the Indians,
Nophaie first appears as the conqueror of the cliff dwellers,
one of whom prophesies that a stronger race will appear to
conquer the Indians. In the next episode of the prologue,
the Spaniards are that stronger race who subdue the Indians
by overcoming the Warrior. Nophaie, seen in an extreme long
shot from a low angle, rides his white horse back and forth
on a high bluff until one shot from a Spanish soldier's gun
knocks him off. His death moves large numbers of Indians,
already weakened by wine, to bow in homage to a few Spaniards. Later, in the final episode set in the early days of
the United States, Kit Carson and U.S. soldiers threaten
Nophaie and his Indians. In this sequence he again rides
his white horse on a high bluff and this time is killed by a
single shot from a cannon positioned far below him. The In-

dians end up, contrary to the promises of Kit Carson, dom-
inated by Indian agents on a reservation where Nophaie appears for the last time as the main character of the film.

On the reservation Nophaie (Richard Dix) meets the
forces that will ultimately destroy him as a symbolic leader of
the Indians, one of which is the Christian religion as represented by Marion, the white schoolteacher he loves, and her
Bible. In one significant scene, Marion reads her Bible to
Nophaie, who is seen from a slight high angle sitting on the
floor at her feet, as she tries to teach him about Christian
self-denial and martyrdom. This scene suggests that the Warrior is less powerful than the white woman and is already
being controlled by her religion. This control is shown fig-
uratively later when a little Bible Marion gave Nophaie prompts
him to save the life of his white rival for Marion during the
war. Later, when Nophaie is trying to pray to his Indian
gods, he looks at the same Bible and decides to invoke the
Christian God. Finally, as he tries to stop the attack of his
people, he is shot in the chest through the little Bible.

In the last part of the film, after Nophaie and the other
Indians return from World War I, they find that the evil Indian agent, Booker, has taken their land and caused the death
of an Indian woman. When the tribe decides to fight for its
rights, Nophaie, described earlier in the film as the Warrior
who "for every generation would do what no one else would
attempt," tries to stop them, but the fighting ends only when
he is fatally wounded by one of his people. While lying on the
ground with Marion holding him in her arms, and an Indian on
either side, he says that he now understands that one who finds
life will lose it and one who loses it will find everlasting life.
The Warrior has become a Christian martyr and only his death
brings peace between the Indians and Whites. Once again
Nophaie does what no other Indian would attempt, but this
act marks the end of the Warrior spirit because it has been
transformed into a Christian action. The final scene is an
extreme long shot of a lengthy procession of Indians vanishing
into the horizon as they carry the body of Nophaie. This
procession and several others earlier in the film form a striking image of the noble but doomed Indian slowly but steadily
being moved out of the picture by the stronger society and
religion of the Whites.

In The Vanishing American and other earlier silent films

this sentimental image of the noble but doomed Indian offers an easy vehicle for expressing sympathy. It also frees the audience from any direct sense of responsibility because it shows that the destruction of Indian culture is the sad but natural result of social evolution to white culture. Also, the audience feels good because, in the typically melodramatic fashion of the silent films, evil has been punished by the death of Booker and virtue has been rewarded through the peace between the Indians and good whites like Marion. Such melodramatic form also provides an easy vehicle for the image of the bloodthirsty Indian, which became more popular later in the silent westerns. Again the audience could feel good about the destruction of the Indian because this image portrayed them as melodramatic villains: vicious, evil enemies who were justly and necessarily conquered.

*   *   *

The following filmography is representative but not exhaustive. From 1910 to 1913 alone, one hundred or more films about Indians appeared each year, and throughout most of the silent period the American Indian remained a very popular subject.

This filmography on the silent film era ends with 1929. The cut-off year is somewhat arbitrary since some films before this date have music, sound effects and some dialogue. A few films after 1929 are still basically silent, but most have music, narration, or dialogue.

NOTE

1. These titles come from representative listings in Spehr. Ralph and Natasha Friar give extensive lists of film titles for the silent era (pp. 287-323 and the early chapters on silent film). The best primary source for plot summaries of silent films dealing with Indians is Moving Picture World (MPW), the first film magazine. Published from 1907 to 1927, this periodical describes many of the Indian films of this era. Finally, the Biograph Bulletin, 1908-1912 provides detailed plot summaries of the early D.W. Griffith films.

1903

1 Kit Carson (American Mutoscope and Biograph 1903)
   Indians follow and attack Kit Carson in a series of
scenes as in a serial. At the end a young Indian woman
rescues him. Claiming that this film is a "novelty" because of its historical accuracy, the Biograph Bulletin refers to part nine, In the Indian Camp: "Squaws and their
papooses, young bucks and Indian maidens are seen at
their various occupations. Here we have real Indian life."
(Niver 215)

2 The Pioneers (American Mutoscope and Biograph 1903)
   Indians attack a family in a cabin, kill the parents and
kidnap the daughter. At the end trappers rescue the
young woman and kill the Indians.

1907

3 Daniel Boone (Edison 1907)
   Indians kidnap Boone's daughters and then capture and
torture him. Finally Boone escapes, rescues his daughters
with the aid of an Indian maiden (who had been treated
well by them earlier), and then kills the chief.

4 Pioneer Days (Edison 1907)
   After Indians take two white children from a cabin,
their father trails them, and with the help of an Indian
woman rescues them.

1908

5 The Call of the Wild (Biograph 1908) D.W. Griffith
   In this film, subtitled "Sad Plight of the Civilized Redman," George Redfeather, a football player from the Carlisle Indian School, proposes to the white woman. When
she declines, he angrily returns to his tribe. Later,
while the woman is riding in the woods, he captures her
and is about to take vengeance when she uses religion to
talk him out of it.

6 In the Days of the Pilgrims (Vitagraph 1908)
   Indians capture a pilgrim and his daughter; later the

young woman tomahawks the chief and escapes with the
help of her white lover.

7   The Justice of the Redskin (Pathé 1908)
    An Indian accused of killing a little girl trails the
actual murderer and, after finding the man with the body
of the child, throws him off a cliff.

8   The Kentuckian (Biograph 1908)
    A rich young man goes West and marries an Indian
woman. As he is struggling whether to return to the East
for his inheritance, his Indian wife understands his dilemma and solves his problem by committing suicide.

9   Pioneers Crossing the Plains in '49 (Pathé 1908)
    After Indians attack covered wagons, carry away a
white girl and capture her lover, the girl escapes and
rescues her lover who had been tied to a wild horse.

10 Pocahontas: A Child of the Forest (Edison 1908)
    Powhatan, the father of Pocahontas, treats Captain
Smith well and agrees to a marriage of the white man and
Pocahontas after she saves Smith from the evil Indian,
Kunder-Wacha. A reviewer in Variety notes the lack of
accuracy: "The Indians in Pocahontas look like Chinese
ballet girls must appear, if they have ballet girls in
China." (3 Oct)

11 The Red Girl (Biograph 1908) D.W. Griffith
    After an Indian woman is tied up and suspended over
a river by her unfaithful half-breed husband and an evil
Mexican woman, a white woman comes to her rescue and
the Indian rejects her husband.

12 The Redman and the Child (Biograph 1908) D.W. Griffith
    In this film, subtitled "The Story of an Indian's Ven-
geance," outlaws kill an old miner and kidnap his grand-
child while their Indian friend (Charles Innslee) is away.
Upon his return, the Indian rescues the child and avenges
the death of his old friend by killing the outlaws. The
Biograph Bulletin describes the Indian as "a magnificent
type of the aboriginal American ... a noble creature, as
kind-hearted as a woman and as brave as a lion...."
(Bowser 5)

13   Under the Star Spangled Banner (Kalem 1908)
     Indians attack an immigrant family in a covered wagon
and are then driven off by U.S. soldiers carrying the
flag.

                              1909

14   Comata, the Sioux (Biograph 1909) D.W. Griffith
     Clear Eyes leaves her village to live with a white man
and they have a child. After the man abandons her for
a white woman, she goes off toward the Black Hills with
Comata (James Kirkwood), who has loved and guarded her
from the beginning, but they both come to a sad end.

15   Hiawatha (Laemmle 1909)
     Based on Longfellow's "The Song of Hiawatha," the
film tells the love story of Hiawatha, an Ojibway, and
Minnehaha, a Sioux, and ends with their marriage. A
Variety reviewer notes that "the actors, both men and
women, seemingly cannot secure the wild natural abandon
of the Indian." (30 Oct)

16   Indian Runner's Romance (Biograph 1909) D.W. Griffith
     After a cowboy kidnaps the wife of Blue Cloud (James
Kirkwood), a Sioux, and tortures her to find the location
of a hidden mine, the Indian kills him and brings his
wife home. A Variety reviewer comments that "'Made up'
Indians are usually a travesty, but in this case both in
appearance and action the redskin is natural." (28 Sept)

17   The Mended Lute (Biograph 1909) D.W. Griffith
     Little Bear and Standing Rock are vying for the Sioux
chief's daughter, Rising Moon, and the chief gives her to
the highest bidder, Standing Rock, the man she doesn't
love. After she leaves her new husband for Little Bear
whom she loves, the two are captured by Standing Rock
and his tribe and are about to be burned at the stake
when, impressed by his rival's bravery, he sets them
both free.

18   On the Little Big Horn (Selig 1909)
     Rain in the Face, who had been arrested earlier by
Custer's brother, takes revenge by leading Custer and
his men to the Little Big Horn river where they are killed
in "The Last Stand." (MPW 27 Nov 773)

19 Pale Face's Wooing (Kalem 1909)
    Little Redheart is caught between her love for a cow-
boy and her father's desire for her to marry an Indian
who has asked for her. After the father and the Indian
capture the cowboy and are about to kill him, she comes
to the rescue. Then, when the cowboy kills the rival Indian and is about to kill her father, Little Redheart inter-
cedes and her father forgives them and agrees to their
marriage. A Variety reviewer notes that such "Indian
subjects are always interesting. They have the freshness
of the wild." (27 Nov)

20 The Red Man (World 1909)
    An Indian repays a white man who helped him earlier
by recovering the man's money from a thief. An MPW
reviewer notes that the film "shows that singular gratitude
of the Indian which was often displayed in these days."
(26 June 884)

21 A Red Man's Love (Columbia 1909)
    An Indian who is betrothed falls in love with a white
woman captured by his tribe and, after rescuing her and
fighting off the pursuing Indians, returns her to her
father's home. He renounces his people and asks for the
white woman's hand in marriage only to be rejected by her
and the family.

22 The Redman's View (Biograph 1909) D.W. Griffith
    Armed and unfeeling whites force reluctant Kiowas to
move from their land farther west. They then allow the
chief's daughter, Minnewanna, whom they have kept behind, to go with Silver Eagle, the young Indian she loves,
to visit the burial site of her father. The Biograph Bulletin notes that the film beautifully depicts the suffering
of Indians who were made "to trek from place to place by
the march of progress which was ever forging its way into the West." (Bowser 149)

23 Red Wing's Gratitude (Vitagraph 1909)
    After white settlers rescue Red Wing (Princess Red-
wing) from a beating by her own people, the Indians kidnap a white girl whom Red Wing then helps to escape.
Though settlers come to their rescue, Red Wing is wounded
by the Indians and dies in the arms of the white girl's
father.

1910

24 A Broken Doll (Biograph 1910) D.W. Griffith
        In this film subtitled "A Tragedy of the Indian Reserva-
    tion," after a villain cruelly kills an Indian, the tribe
    prepares to take revenge and an Indian girl who had re-
    ceived a doll from a white child shows her gratitude by
    warning the whites, only to be killed in the fighting.

25 Cheyenne Brave (Pathé 1910)
        Two Indians duel for the hand of an Indian girl; her
    lover wins and takes her to the land of his people. An
    MPW reviewer calls the film "one of the most, if not the
    most, remarkable Indian pictures ever produced.... All
    the actors taking part in this picture are real Indians or
    sufficiently well made up to pass as such." (6 Aug 299)

26 Cheyenne Raiders (Kalem 1910)
        In an article, "Kalem Indian Stories Popular," an MPW
    reviewer explains that the historical accuracy of this film
    is typical of Kalem productions in which the directors
    were provided "an understanding of the customs of the
    particular tribe of Indians gathered from the most authori-
    tative sources." (6 June 1099)

27 Days of the Early West (Champion 1910)
        Soon after two religious pioneer families build a cabin,
    Indians attack and set the cabin on fire. At the last
    moment, townspeople arrive and rescue them.

28 A Frontier Hero (Edison 1910)
        Indians attack pioneer families as they try to settle
    the frontier in the 1840's. An MPW reviewer notes that
    such Indian attacks were a constant threat to the pioneers,
    a "menace" that the film "illustrates graphically." (6
    Aug 296)

29 The Heart of a Sioux (Lubin 1910)
        An Indian girl falls in love with her white teacher
    and, though the love is unrequited, she saves his life
    twice. A reviewer for MPW argues that the movies are
    showing that Indians, contrary to the stereotype of them
    as "stolid, unemotional people," experience strong emo-
    tions like love and hate. He believes that this film will
    "go far to remove the stigma which this oft-repeated as-

sertion, that Indians lack heart, has placed upon the
race." (20 Aug 365)

30 The Indian Land Grab (Champion 1910)
      A young Indian sent by his people to fight against land
grabbing by a crooked white politician fails to stop the
passage of the politician's bill because the white man's
daughter tricks him. After the Indian returns to his
tribe and is about to be executed for his failure, the
woman, who has repented and recognized her love for the
Indian, appears with a document protecting the Indian
land. At the end they are married and live among his
people.

31 The Indian Scout's Revenge (Kalem 1910)
      Incited by a Mexican villain, Indians attack a wagon
train and capture an Indian scout's girl. The scout gets
revenge by killing the Mexican and the Indians.

32 Indian Squaw's Sacrifice (Defender 1910)
      After Noweeta finds a wounded white man, nurses him
back to health, marries and has a child with him, the man
meets a white woman he had loved earlier. When Noweeta
realizes that her husband still loves the woman, she goes
off to the woods and kills herself so that they can marry.

33 A Kentucky Pioneer (Selig 1910)
      After an Indian kidnaps a white woman betrothed to a
settler, she escapes with the help of a young Indian woman
and the settlers rescue her from the pursuing Indians. A
Variety critic notes that this is "a theme displayed many
times before." (8 Oct)

34 Kit Carson (Bison 1910)
      The hero rescues some settlers from an Indian attack.
An MPW critic comments that the film has all the "features
of the old time frontier story" including a "surrounding
band of whooping redskins, showering arrows into the
stockade." (10 Sept 575)

35 Lo, the Poor Indian (Kalem 1910)
      An Indian who has stolen a horse to save his wife and
child is in jail because of laws he doesn't understand. An
MPW reviewer notes that the film "should arouse a sense
of the injustice which has been meted out to unfortunate

Indians on the supposed intention of following the white
man's ideas of justice." (9 April 553)

36 The Maid of Niagara (Pathé 1910)
    When his beloved Red Doe is sacrificed to the Spirit
    of the Falls, a young Iroquois, Esoomget, drowns himself
    in the river so he will be with his bride in the next world.

37 A Mohawk's Way (Biograph 1910) D.W. Griffith
    An Indian woman rescues a white woman, who had
    earlier saved her baby, as she is about to be killed by
    Indians who had been wronged by the white woman's
    evil husband. A contemporary reviewer notes that the
    Indian in the film is "the noble red man of James Feni-
    more Cooper...the Indian of romance who, as some people
    claim, never existed, but who is nevertheless the ideal
    type for story telling." (Friar 117)

38 Pocahontas (Thanhouser 1910)
    After Pocahontas has saved the life of Captain John
    Smith, she is captured by the English and eventually
    marries John Rolfe, with whom she goes to England. Not
    too long after her arrival she dies dreaming of her na-
    tive wilderness.

39 Ramona (Biograph 1910) D.W. Griffith
    In this film subtitled "A Story of the Whiteman's In-
    justice to the Indian," Ramona suffers because of her
    marriage to Alessandro, the Indian. A reviewer for MPW,
    commenting on how the film follows closely the romantic
    novel of the same name written by Helen Hunt Jackson,
    writes that the film is worthwhile because it shows "graph-
    ically the injustice which preceded the settlement of a con-
    siderable proportion of the United States." (4 June 942)

40 Red Wing's Loyalty (Bison 1910)
    A lieutenant helps Red Wing, who has been hurt by
    an evil half-breed, but so intent on finding the Indian
    gold he later kills her father, the Chief. Later the In-
    dians capture the lieutenant and are about to burn him at
    the stake when Red Wing brings the soldiers who drive
    off the Indians and reward Red Wing for her loyalty to
    the lieutenant.

41 Riders of the Plains (Edison 1910)

Canadian Northwest Mounted Police follow Indians who have stolen horses hundreds of miles before they capture them and put them in prison. An MPW reviewer notes that "the Edison Co. takes considerable pride because the participants are not make believe actors ... the Indians are real Indians...." (12 Nov 1125)

42   A Romance of the Western Hills (Biograph 1910) D.W. Griffith

A young Indian woman, adopted by a white family, falls in love with a white man who cruelly rejects her. She meets an Indian who had loved her earlier and returns to avenge her rejection, then goes to her tribe with her lover. The Biograph Bulletin describes the film as a "powerful illustration of one of the many indignities the redskin suffered." (Bowser 185)

43   Song of the Wildwood Flute (Biograph 1910) D.W. Griffith

After hearing him play the flute, Dove Eyes (Mary Pickford) chooses to marry Gray Cloud (Chief Dark Cloud) rather than another Indian suitor. When Gray Cloud falls into a bear pit, his rival, who sees the maiden's suffering, shows his honor by rescuing him. A Variety reviewer notes that the "poor attempt by the principal characters to act as Indians is pitiable." (3 Dec)

44   A Trapper and the Redskins (Kalem 1910)

After Indians carry off the daughter and capture her father, a trapper, her mother and their neighbors rescue the two and kill all the Indians. A Variety reviewer writes "the band [of Indians] is killed off in fine stockyard order and everything ends happily except for the poor Indians." (26 Feb)

45   A True Indian Brave (Bison 1910)

When some settlers insult an Indian woman and her Indian lover defends her, they try to lynch the two Indians. An MPW critic comments that the filmmaker gave "a truer picture than he intended. He may have shown why some of the difficulties between the whites and Indians began ... and the conclusions will not be wholly flattering to the white man." (23 Sept 689)

<u>1911</u>

46   The American Insurrecto (Kalem 1911)
        An Indian woman, who cares for a wounded American
soldier of fortune and helps him escape his enemies,
finally leaves him to marry an Indian chief.

47   Curse of the Red Man (Selig 1911)
        An educated Indian struggles with alcoholism after he
returns from college to live with his tribe.

48   Flaming Arrows (Pathé 1911)
        Indians trap a frontier party in a cabin and shoot
flaming arrows to smoke them out.

49   In the Days of the Six Nations (Republic 1911)
        After a treacherous Indian guide leads a lieutenant and
two women into a trap, a well-known trapper rescues them.
Later, when the Indians finally capture the women and
are about to kill the lieutenant, the trapper brings soldiers
who drive off the Indians.

50   Indian Brothers (Biograph 1911) D.W. Griffith
        In this film subtitled "The Story of an Indian's Honor,"
after a renegade Indian kills a sick chief, the chief's
brother captures the man and punishes him for the murder.

51   The Last of the Mohicans (Thanhouser 1911)
        This version of Cooper's novel follows the original plot
quite closely, right down to the scene in which Heywood
and Hawkeye, disguised as a medicine man and his trained
bear, rescue one of the daughters of Colonel Monro.

52   Little Dove's Romance (Bison 1911)
        Little Dove falls in love with a white man, but after the
man explains that he cannot marry her, she agrees to marry her Indian lover. An MPW reviewer comments that the
film shows "something of Indian manners and customs ...
in a way that shows a sympathetic understanding of the
Indian mind." (9 Sept 692)

53   Love in a Tepee (Imperial 1911)
        An Indian named Bad Eye wants his daughter, Hyacinth,
who loves a cowboy, to marry a Mexican.   The Mexican

thinks that Bad Eye, who is laying under the blanket in a drunken stupor, is the daughter and carries him away.

54 The Maiden of the Pie-Faced Indians (Edison 1911)
    After the maiden is captured, the Indians catch the hero and torture him before he is rescued. An MPW reviewer, noting that the hero walks away with the tree to which he was tied, comments that the film "clearly illustrates the absurdities which often creep into the usual Indian story." (7 Oct 129)

55 The Mesquite's Gratitude (Kalem 1911)
    After a cowboy stops other ranch hands from taunting a young Indian woman, Mesquite, she helps him and later he comes to the Indian camp and asks to marry her.

56 Ogallah (Powers 1911)
    A Sioux pursues a kidnapper and finally takes his vengeance by killing him. An MPW reviewer comments that the film has "no mawkish sentimentality.... It is savage and cruel, as Indians are by nature." (18 April 782)

57 A Prisoner of the Mohicans (Pathé 1911)
    After Mohicans capture a white girl who had earlier helped a poor, starving Indian, he shows his gratitude by rescuing her from the Mohican camp and returning her to her parents.

58 The Red Man's Penalty (Bison 1911)
    After they were given rotten meat by a mean and crooked Indian agent, Indians attack and capture two whites. The cavalry then attacks them and they are heavily and unjustly punished.

59 The Squaw's Love (Biograph 1911) D.W. Griffith
    White Eagle (Chief Dark Cloud), who is betrothed to Silver Fawn, helps his exiled friend Gray Fox by bringing Wild Flower, Gray Fox's lover, to meet him in the forest. Silver Fawn, who sees the two and thinks that Wild Flower is after White Eagle, throws her in the river. Gray Fox rescues his lover and, after the four understand the situation, they all escape from hostile Indians who are pursuing them. Along with films like The Legend of Scarface (1910), A Sioux Spy (1911), and An Indian Idyl (1912) this film is a good example of many films that dealt exclusively with Indian life.

60 The Totem Mark (Selig 1911)
        Indians kidnap a white woman and a group of Indian
    women, jealous of her beauty, denounce her as a witch
    and set her adrift in the rapids of a river.

61 Yaqui Girl (Pathé 1911) James Young Deer
        Directed by a successful Indian director for Pathé,
    this film deals with unrequited love. An Indian girl falls
    in love with a Mexican singer who not only turns out to
    be a bandit but also loves another woman.

                                    1912

62 At Old Fort Dearborn (Bison 1912) Frank Monty
        Singing Bird (Mona Darkfeather) loves a white soldier
    and is slain by her tribe as she helps him escape. An
    MPW reviewer comments that "Little Mona Darkfeather ...
    has a role that will prove to be a popular one--that of a
    friend of the soldiers." (28 Sept 1267)

63 Chief White Eagle (Lubin 1912)
        White Eagle, a young Indian educated in the East, re-
    turns to take the leadership of his tribe after he had
    killed a white woman who cruelly rejected his love. A re-
    luctant white man hunts him down and, after he has killed
    White Eagle, prays for him as do the members of his tribe.

64 Custer's Last Fight (Bison 1912) Thomas Ince
        This film depicts Custer's (Francis Ford) battle with
    the Sioux at Little Big Horn. An MPW reviewer, who be-
    lieves that all the writers and filmmakers who created the
    "Noble Redman" ought to be made to fight or live with the
    Indians, argues that Indians are "merciless to the weak,
    inhuman in their outrages upon white women and children
    and ... incapable of gratitude...." (22 June 1118)

65 Early Days in the West (Bison 1912)
        After a white woman rejects the love of Mahomena, the
    Indian leading her wagon train, and her white lover further
    punishes him, he gains his revenge by helping the hostile
    Sioux attack the wagon train. Two other examples of an
    Indian man rejected by a white woman who will then either
    kill her or attack whites in revenge are Indian Blood (1913)
    and Burning Brand (1913).

66 The Fall of Black Hawk (American 1912) William Lee
      This film deals with the Sauk and Fox tribes led by
    Black Hawk. An MPW reviewer comments that this picture
    depicts "those stirring events which led to the wanton
    slaughter of countless white settlers." (20 July 776)

67 Forest Rose (Thanhouser 1912)
      Indians attack a pioneer and kidnap his daughter.
    This film provokes Louis R. Harrison of MPW to comment
    that "there is very little that can be truthfully represented
    as ideal in the character of a people gloating over hideous
    torture of innocent women and children. They represent
    a hindering and utterly useless element in the civilization
    of humankind." (30 Nov 861)

68 Geronimo's Last Raid (American 1912) John Emerson
      Geronimo's Apaches attack and capture the hero and
    as he is about to be burned at the stake, he is rescued
    by his beloved when she shoots three Indians by firing
    through the bung-hole of a barrel. An MPW reviewer
    notes that "there is action and lots of it, for those who
    like clashes between Indians and settlers and who are
    stirred by the dashing attacks of the U.S. Cavalry and
    cowboys on the redskins." (14 Sept 1054)

69 Indian Massacre (Bison 1912) Thomas Ince
      A film historian explains that this film shows "the quest
    of the white settlers for land in their westward movement,
    as well as the plight of the Indian as a result of this mi-
    gration. The final scene shows a silhouette of an Indian
    woman praying by her dead child's grave." (Parish 158)

70 Indian Romeo and Juliet (Vitagraph 1912)
      The story of an ill-fated love between a young man and
    woman from the warring Huron and Mohican tribes.

71 The Invaders (Kay-Bee 1912)
      Chief Eagleshirt and his Sioux attack and kill some
    surveyors who have entered their land. At the end, Sky
    Star (Ann Little), who loved one of the surveyors, dies
    and reinforcements arrive to drive off the Indians who
    are attacking the fort.

72 Iola's Promise (Biograph 1912) D.W. Griffith
      In this film subtitled "How the Little Indian Maiden

Paid Her Debt of Gratitude"; after a kind prospector helps
Iola (Mary Pickford), she rescues his fiancée as her tribe
is about to burn her at the stake. In the rescue, Iola
is fatally wounded but she manages to tell the prospector
where some gold is before she dies.

73 The Little Indian Martyr (Selig 1912)
      The rebellious Indians of the mission make Chiquito,
a boy who works for a kindly priest, promise that he will
kill the priest, but Chiquito warns him, only to be killed
as the Indians shoot into the room.

74 The Massacre (Biograph 1912) D.W. Griffith
      Indians circle a wagon train and kill everyone but a
young woman and her child before the cavalry drives them
off. The attack on the small group of people seems to
parallel that on Custer at Little Big Horn, though the
Biograph Bulletin notes the "film depicts the struggles of
the early settlers in the Northwest in their conflict with
the fierce Indian tribes of that time." (MPW 14 Feb 1914)

75 On the Warpath (Bison-101 1912)
      An old Indian dreams of ancient battles in which Apaches
struggle with peace-loving Yumas and of a romance between a man of one tribe and a woman of the other.

76 A Pueblo Legend (Biograph 1912) D.W. Griffith
      After the high priest tells of a turquoise stone which
fell from the heavens and would bring wealth and happiness to the tribe, one of its leaders is chosen to journey
out and find the stone. An MPW reviewer, quoting the
Biograph Bulletin, notes that the film is "a most beautiful
portrayal of early Indian symbolism." (24 May 790)

77 The Red Man's Honor (Eclipse 1912) Gaston Roudes
      Though innocent, Red Hawk is convicted of killing
Seated Bear, who had been his rival for the love of June
Dew, and is sentenced by Chief Red Hawk to be executed
one year later. Red Hawk shows his honor by returning
at the time appointed for his death and his beloved June
Dew dies with him.

78 The Tribal Law (Bison 1912) Otis Turner
      A Hopi Indian maiden, Starlight, and an Apache man,
José Seville, a graduate of Carlisle, marry despite a Hopi

law against such a match. When Starlight's jilted lover,
Gray Wolf, tries to get them killed, Crouching Panther,
a friendly Hopi man that José had helped earlier, rescues
them. An MPW reviewer praises the film because it is not
"of the orthodox sort--burning, raiding, soldiers to the
rescue, and all of the regular program. It is a story of
Indians as Indians, and in it are shown the habitations,
the mode of life, some of the customs." (9 Nov 536)

79 The Vanishing Race (American 1912)
     An Indian family, the last of the "Hoppe" tribe, get
caught in a circle of revenge as the brother kills a white
man who rejects his sister. The whites then kill the
brother and father, leaving only the mother and daughter
to wander away.

                          1913

80 The Battle at Elderbush Gulch (Biograph 1913) D.W. Grif-
    fith
     After a white man kills the son of the chief, the In-
dians kill settlers, including women and babies, and threat-
en a mother and baby hiding in a cabin until soldiers ar-
rive and rescue the two.

81 Call of the Blood (Cinemacolor 1913)
     Indians attack pioneers in a covered wagon and kidnap
a pregnant mother. When she dies her new daughter
grows up with the Indians. Years later a young captain
in the army competes with an Indian for the girl's love
but finds out she is his long-lost sister.

82 Deerslayer (Vitagraph 1913)
     Cooper's heroes, Natty Bumppo and his friend Chinga-
chgook, fight the Hurons. An MPW reviewer, tired of the
"scalping knife" and "war paint and feather bonnets" of
contemporary movies, welcomes this revival of Cooper.
(5 April 31)

83 The Friendless Indian (Pathé 1913)
     An Indian rejected by his own people twice rescues a
little white girl but is also rejected by the whites. An
MPW reviewer comments: "Condemned to walk alone, a
Red Man saves a life and is given only a nod for thanks--
after all, he is Indian." (12 July 232)

84 Heart of an Indian (Bison 1913) Thomas Ince
        An Indian chief (J.B. Sherry) steals a white baby to
    replace the dead child of his daughter (Ann Little) but
    she, seeing how much the mother loves the baby, gives
    it back. In the meantime, the whites, not knowing about
    this, kill many of the Indians in revenge. At the end
    the few survivors perform burial rituals.

85 Hiawatha (Moore 1913) F.E. Moore
        This adaptation of Longfellow's epic poem about the
    love of Hiawatha and Minnehaha uses all Indian actors.
    An MPW reviewer praises the acting of the Indians and
    the subject matter of the film and comments, "we have had
    such a fearful surfeit of blood thirsty Indians, scalping
    Indians, howling Indians, gambling Indians and murdering
    and burning Indians in the cheap films, that it was like
    a breath of fresh air to see real human Indians enacting
    before us an old Indian legend.... While in the ordinary
    Indian film the red men shout and gesticulate like a lot of
    excited French, the Indians of these reels show all that
    stoic and impressive calm which the white man has never
    been quite able to understand." (8 Mar 980)

86 In the Long Ago (Selig 1913) Colin Campbell
        A young Indian revives his lover, Starlight, who has
    been under a spell, by playing a wind pipe made from
    the thigh bone of a great chief. These legendary lovers
    are then compared to two modern ones.

87 On Fortune's Wheel (Kay Bee 1913)
        In Arizona, Indians capture a banker who has been
    cheating them on land deals, and they gain their revenge
    by tying him to a wagon wheel and burning him.

88 The Yaqui Cur (Biograph 1913) D.W. Griffith
        A young Yaqui (Robert Herron), who learns white cus-
    toms like smoking cigarettes and reading the Bible, later
    refuses to fight with his people when they attack the
    whites, is exiled from the tribe but finally gives his life
    for the Indian woman he had loved and lost.

                              1914

89 The Indian Servant (Great Northern 1914)

In this comedy, which makes the Indian the butt of
the humor, a foreign diplomat brings home an Indian to
be his servant. The Indian takes bonnets from the heads
of three young women in a millinery shop, improperly
woos the maids, paints himself and the children, war
dances with them and almost wrecks the house.

90 The Indian Wars (Col. Wm. F. Cody Historical Pictures
1914)
     This famous film produced by William F. Cody chron-
icles the major Indian battles. An MPW reviewer advises
his readers to take a young person to the film "for an
afternoon with the great leaders of our army, with the
great chiefs of our Indian tribes and two hours in the
open world that has been made sacred by heroic blood of
the nation's fighting heroes." (12 Sept 1500) For an extended discussion and pictures from the film, most of
which are no longer extant, see Brownlow, pp. 224-235.

91 Last of the Line (Bison 1914) Jay Hunt
     After studying at a white college, the son of Chief
Gray Otter (William Eagleshirt) returns to his Sioux tribe
a hopeless drunk. After he and some renegades break
the peace made by Gray Otter, the Chief must kill him
but does it in a way that makes him look like a hero to
the soldiers.

92 Perils of Pauline (Pathé 1914) Donald McKenzie
     In this most famous of the early serials, the Indians
at first accept Pauline as a goddess and then roll a huge
boulder down a hill at her to see if she is immortal.

93 Renegade's Sister (Miller Bros. 1914)
     After a white man steals cattle and horses from the
Indians, they pursue him over great distances and finally
gain vengeance by killing him.

94 Rose of the Rancho (Lasky 1914)
     Based on a popular contemporary play, this film has a
villain who is a ferocious half-breed (William Elmer).

95 The Squaw Man (Paramount 1914) Cecil B. De Mille
     Based on the play by Edwin M. Royle, this film deals
with an Englishman who marries Nat-U-Rich (Princess Redwing), the daughter of the Ute Chief Tabywana (Joe

Singleton), who twice rescues him when he is in trouble.
When she finds out that her son must go to England and
that her husband loves an Englishwoman, she kills herself to free them.

96 Strongheart (Biograph 1914)
      Based on a well-known contemporary play, this film
has a hero named Strongheart who leaves his tribe, goes
to college in the East, becomes a football star, gets in
trouble for lying to help a white friend who has cheated,
and falls in love with a white woman. When he finds out
that his tribe needs him because of the death of his
father, he respects his duty and, leaving his sweetheart
behind, sadly returns to his people.

97 The Thundering Herd (Selig 1914)
      After Indians led by Chief Swift Wing (Wheeler Oak-
man) attack and capture the hero and his sweetheart,
Swift Wing wants the white woman but Starlight (Princess
Redwing) befriends the captives and rescues them several
times. After harrowing adventures with buffalo hunters
and Indians, they reach their homeland with Starlight as
their companion. A Variety reviewer comments that "the
former kings of the plains are also permitted to run into
the range of the camera fire occasionally and help lengthen
out the feature." (6 Aug 1915)

98 The Virginian (Lasky 1914)
      Indian attacks fill out the plot of this film. A Variety
reviewer comments on the comic lack of reality in one of
the Indian fights when the hero, who is badly wounded,
"spies an Indian several hundred feet away and shoots
left handed from his hip with fatal effect." (11 Sept)

99 Where the Trail Divides (Lasky 1914)
      An Indian named How (Robert Edeson) marries a white
woman but then releases her so she can live in comfort in
the East with a white man who turns out to be a villain.
Eventually How brings her back to the West and, after
the husband dies committing a crime, the two renew their
love. A Variety reviewer comments: "Mr. Edeson looked
more like a negro than an Indian ... his make-up was de-
cidedly black. Whatever sympathy the average auditor
holds for the Indian was lost through this." (17 Oct)

100   The Winner (Box Office Attraction G. 1914)
      The hero is blamed for killing a cowboy who was ac-
tually shot by a half-breed he had cheated and ridiculed.
The half-breed shows his honor by sending a letter ad-
mitting the act.

1915

101   From Out of the Big Snows (Vitagraph 1915)
      When Jean La Salle (George Cooper), a half-breed,
finds out that his white lover is infatuated with a doctor,
he seeks his revenge by tying the man to a tree to be
eaten by wolves. A Variety reviewer describes the
character as a "half-breed, who with inborn cunning,
professes a friendship for the white man so that he may
later dispose of him." (13 Aug)

102   The Ghost Wagon (Bison 1915)
      After a white girl, whose parents were killed by In-
dians, is abducted by an evil half-breed and then rescued
by her lover, the half-breed retaliates by inciting the
Indians to attack the settlement.

103   Neola, the Sioux (Exposition Players Corp. and 101 Ranch
      1915)
      A white man, who raped Neola (Neola May) and is
forced to marry her, finally abandons her in San Fran-
cisco. Red Deer (Pedro Leon) finds her and takes her
to the Sioux tribe which has joined the 101 Ranch Western Show. Later, Red Deer kills Neola's evil husband
and he and Neola pledge their love to each other.

104   The Sealed Valley (Metro 1915)
      An Indian girl, Nahnya Crossfox (Dorothy Donnelly)
lives with her parents in a sealed valley full of gold
called Indian's Paradise. After falling in love with a
white doctor but deciding he should have a white woman
rather than herself and foiling an attempt by a half-breed
to get the gold, Nahnya seals herself in the valley to
live the rest of her life alone.

1916

105   The Aryan (Triangle 1916)

The hero (W.S. Hart), a woman-hater, finally decides
to rescue a wagon train from his own gang of renegade
Indians and half-breeds when a woman convinces him
that white men must protect the women of their Aryan
race from the Indians.

106   The Bugle Call (Triangle 1916) Reginald Barker
      After diverting the main troops by a clever deception,
the Indians attack the fort but they, in turn, are tricked
into thinking the troops are returning by a boy who plays
the bugle call.

107   The Captive God (Triangle 1916) Thomas Ince
      Chaipa (W.S. Hart), a Spaniard adopted by peaceful
cliff-dwelling Indians, and some warriors escape after an
Aztec attack. The Aztecs finally capture Chaipa and
are about to kill him when his lover Lolomi (Enid Markey),
the daughter of Montezuma, the Aztec's chief, arrives
with his warriors and rescues him. A Variety reviewer
notes that "The story is one of the type that has long
held sway in the popular fiction magazines, it is at once
thrilling and carries an air of mystic romance that is
compelling." (7 July)

108   Dawn Maker (Triangle 1916)
      Joe Elk (W.S. Hart), a half-breed who falls in love
with a white woman and struggles over whether to be
loyal to his white or Indian values, decides to fight
against the Indians led by Chief Trouble Thunder (Joe
Goodboy) to rescue the white woman and her white lover.
At the end he accepts his Indian ways by doing the
dance of The Dawn Maker before he dies.

109   Gold and the Woman (William Fox Vampire Productions
      1916)
      After a white man kills Chief Duskara (Chief Black
Eagle), Duskara's wife (Julia Hurley) puts a curse on
his family that lasts for generations. Years later Leelo
Duskara (C.B. Harkess), the great, great grandson of
the Chief and a Harvard student, falls in love with a
white woman affected by the curse.

110   The Half-Breed (Triangle 1916) Allan Dawn
      Based on a story by Bret Harte, this film deals with
Lo Dorman (Douglas Fairbanks, Sr.) the son of an Indian

woman who had been seduced by a white settler. He
spends his early years as an orphan in the forest after
whites drive him from town. Later he is rejected by
one white woman and then finds happiness with another.

111 Lone Star (1916) Edward Sloman
An Indian (William Russell) who gains fame as a
surgeon is scorned by Indians for following white ways
and by whites because he is an Indian. The film is "a
strong tale of Indian life on the Nebraska reservation."
(Brownlow 329)

112 Ramona (Clune 1916) Donald Crisp
This is the second version of Helen Hunt Jackson's
novel about the tragic love of Ramona (Adda Gleason)
and Alessandro (Monroe Salisbury). A Variety reviewer
notes that "this production has a dramatic and human
appeal that should make it more popular than Miss Jackson's novel--and that had a circulation of over 5 million."
(25 Feb) Another Variety review in the same year notes
that the film is "a plea for justice for the red man who
has been robbed of his land by the constant encroach-
ment of the American on his vested domain." (7 April)

113 The Yaqui (Bluebird 1916)
After Tambor (Hobart Bosworth), the Chief of the
Yaqui, loses his wife and child to Mexican slave dealers,
he rallies his tribe to wreak vengeance on the Mexicans.
A Variety reviewer comments on the production: "Genu-
ine natives were judiciously employed and there is a
wealth of atmospheric detail." (17 Mar)

1917

114 Captain of Gray Horse Troup (Vitagraph 1917) William
Wolbert
Ranchers pull strings in Washington to steal land from
the Indians, one of whom is Crawling Elk (Otto Lederer).
A Variety reviewer notes, "Instead of making all 'Injuns'
merely firewater drinkers, it places them in the attitude
of being the abused nation." (18 May)

115 The Conqueror (Standard 1917) Raoul Walsh
Sam Houston, who spent his youth with the Cherokee,

goes back to the tribe when he doubts his wife's love.
William Eagle Shirt, Chief Birdhead and Little Bear play
Indian chiefs.

116 The Danger Trail (Selig 1917) Frederick A. Thompson
      A half-breed, Jean Croisset (W. Lawson Butt), res-
cues a white woman and falls in love with her, but he
finally decides to let her return to her white lover.

117 The Hidden Children (Metro 1917) Oscar Apfel
      After a young white man is adopted by the Mohicans
and becomes the blood brother to Mayaro (Henry Herbert),
a sagamore, he rescues the mother of his sweetheart from
the Iroquois, killing Amochol (George MacDaniel), their
chief. At the end he and his beloved go through the
Indian ceremony of the "White Bridal."

118 The Red Woman (World 1917) E. Mason Hopper
      The daughter of an Indian chief, Maria Temosach
(Gail Kane), gains high honors at an eastern college but
returns to her tribe in New Mexico because she isn't
accepted by eastern society. Later, after a rich white
man, whose life she has saved and with whom she has a
child, leaves her, she struggles until he returns and
marries her.

119 The Savage (Bluebird 1917) Rupert Julian
      The savage is a half-breed, Julio Sandoval (Monroe
Salisbury) who carries off the white heroine, then changes
his mind, and finally, as he is bringing her home, gives
his life to rescue her white lover.

120 The Squaw Man's Son (Lasky 1917) E.J. Le Saint
      An English half-breed (Wallace Reid), married to a
woman in England, returns alone to America to live with
his tribe and falls in love with Wa-na-gi (Anita King),
a Carlisle graduate who is teaching at the Indian agency.
When she finds out about the wife of her beloved, she
is about to commit suicide. However, the wife's death
allows her to marry the half-breed.

121 Wild and Woolly (Artcraft 1917) John Emerson
      In this comedy, the hero (Douglas Fairbanks, Sr.)
becomes an Indian fighter. A Variety critic comments:
"You've got to laugh when the hero rides into the midst

of a bunch of drunken Indians, swings the girl on the back of his horse and makes a getaway without being shot." (22 June)

122 The Woman God Forgot (Paramount 1917) Cecil B. De Mille
     Tecza (Geraldine Farrar), the daughter of the Aztec Chief Montezuma (Raymond Hatton), is in a love triangle with an officer of Cortez's whom she loves, and Guatemoco (T. Kosloff), a nephew of Montezuma's, whom he wants her to marry. To save her white lover from death, she brings the Spaniards to kill all the Aztecs. At the end she is reunited with her lover.

1918

123 Baree, Son of Kazan (Vitagraph 1918) David Smith
     In the Canadian Northwest, Nepeese (Nell Shipman), a beautiful half-breed woman, who is rescued from the villain by the wolf-dog, Baree, finally marries a white newspaper man.

124 Closin' In (Triangle 1918) J.W. McLaughlin
     This film is one of many in this period dealing with half-breeds in Northwestern Canada. A Variety reviewer comments on a female character, "she looks the typical half-breed ... has the lack of facial expression which is characteristic of most of the French half-breeds up in the far northwest, yet with it all, is good looking." (28 June)

125 The Goddess of Lost Lake (Paralta 1918)
     According to Indian legend, whoever gives a life for that of an Indian killed at the lake long ago will inherit the gold at the bottom. After the father of the half-breed heroine gives his life to Eagle (Frank Lanning), one of many Indians who have waited at the lake since the original killing, she inherits the gold and marries an Englishman.

126 Hands Up (Pathé 1918) James W. Horne
     In this serial, a white woman throws some Inca warriors off a train; they eventually capture her and thinking she is a goddess, are about to offer her as sacrifice to the sun god when she is rescued.

127 Huck and Tom (Paramount 1918) William D. Taylor
      The killing of a doctor by Injun Joe (Frank Lanning)
is the focal point of this film based on Twain's The Adventures of Tom Sawyer.

128 Laughing Bill Hyde (Goldwyn 1918) Hobart Henley
      Bill Hyde (Will Rogers) falls in love with Ponotah
(Anna Lehr), a half-breed, and gets back a mine she
had been cheated out of and they marry.

129 The Man Above the Law (Triangle 1918) Raymond Wells
      A white man married to an Indian woman named Natchah
(Claire McDowell) sells rum to the Indians until a schoolteacher persuades him to stop and take his wife and
child, Tonah (May Geracia), away from the town.

130 The Red Red Heart (Bluebird 1918) Wilfred Lucas
      After Kut-Le (Monroe Salisbury), a young Indian edu-
cated at an eastern university, falls in love with a white
woman, he takes her into the mountains against her will,
during which time she falls in love with him. At the
end they are about to be married.

131 The Sign Invisible (First National 1918) Edgar Lewis
      Lone Deer (Mitchell Lewis), a half-breed separated
from his beloved Winona, is wounded in a fight to save
a white woman and loses his sight. At the end he is
reunited with Winona who cares for him.

132 The Squaw Man (Paramount 1918) Cecil B. De Mille
      In this second of three versions directed by De Mille,
Naturich (Ann Little), the daughter of Tabywana (Noah
Beery, Sr.), marries an Englishman and eventually commits suicide to allow her son and husband to return to
England. A Variety reviewer praises Ann Little's "wonderful characterization of the female redskin with her ex-
pressionless features, changing little in suffering or joy."
He also comments that she displays the "stealth of the
Indian" as she protects her man by shooting the villain,
an act "done in a cool and calculating manner, just as
an Indian would do it." (8 Nov)

133 Tiger Man (W.S. Hart Productions 1918) W.S. Hart
      Apaches attack a wagon train and threaten the life of
the hero.

1919

134 The Brute Breaker (Universal 1919) Lynn F. Reynolds
     About this adventure set in the Canadian forests, a
Variety reviewer comments: "There are a number of
'real Indians' which adds to the picturesqueness of the
scenes and also to the interest of the story." (7 Nov)

135 Desert Gold (Pathé 1919) T. Hayes Hunter
     Based on the Zane Grey novel, this film has a strik-
ing scene in which a Yaqui (W. Lawson Butt) and a
bandit chief struggle on the edge of a cliff. Other Indian characters are a Papago Indian mother (Mrs. Dark
Cloud) and her son (Frank Lanning).

136 A Fight for Love (Universal 1919) John Ford
     After an evil half-breed (Joseph Harris) kills an In-
dian in a fight over an Indian woman and the hero is
blamed for the crime, he hunts down the half-breed and
throws him off a cliff.

137 The Heart of Wetona (Select 1919) Sidney Franklin
     Based on the play by George Scarborough, this film
deals with Wetona (Norma Talmadge), a Blackfoot who
has lost her virginity to a cowardly young white man.
Her father, Chief Quannah, gains his vengeance by
killing the man and Wetona marries the good Indian agent.
A Variety reviewer notes that the film makes "one grave
error" because Wetona, educated in a seminary, uses
"the stilted manner in which Indians speak English."
(10 Jan)

138 Riders of Vengeance (Universal 1919) John Ford
     The hero rescues a schoolteacher from a stagecoach
being attacked by Apaches and later saves a wounded
man during another Apache attack.

139 Told in the Hills (Paramount 1919) George Melford
     In this picture filmed on the Nez Percé reservation,
the hero is suspected of conspiring with Indians, three
of whom are Skulking Brave (Jack Herbert), Kalctan
(Monte Blue) and Talapa (Margaret Lommis).

140 Wagon Tracks (Artcraft 1919) Lambert Hillyer
     Indians threaten a wagon train. A Variety reviewer

comments on such a standard use of Indians: "to form
a climax, Indians are dragged in." (15 Aug)

141 What Am I Bid? (Universal 1919) Robert Z. Leonard
     Dark Cloud (Chief Dark Cloud) is the companion of
the villain. A Variety critic notes that "Chief Dark
Cloud as 'Dark Cloud,' Big Bill's scheming side kick, did
good work. He is a real Indian, and reveals unusual
plasticity of countenance for a son of the forests." (25
April)

1920

142 Behold My Wife (Paramount 1920) George Melford
     In this film based on Gilbert Parker's novel, The
Translation of a Savage, an Englishman marries a half-
breed Indian woman named Lali (Mabel J. Scott) to get
back at his family and sends her to England. After
learning British manners and giving birth to a son, Lali
is eventually reunited with her husband who has come to
realize her worth.

143 The Last of His People (Select 1920) Robert North Bradbury
     Wolf (Mitchell Lewis), an Indian raised by a white man,
eventually falls in love with the man's daughter.

144 The Last of the Mohicans (Associated Producers 1920)
Maurice Tourneur
     In this version of Cooper's novel, Hawkeye (Harry
Lorraine) and his friends Chingachgook (Theodore Lerch)
and his son, Uncas (Albert Roscoe), struggle with the
evil Huron, Magua (Wallace Beery). At the end Magua
kills Uncas and the white woman he loves and Hawkeye
kills Magua. A Variety critic comments on one of the
Indian attacks: "However, someone gets firewater to the
redskins and they take part in an orgy of blood and suggested rapine that was terrible enough in print but becomes unspeakable in a picture." (7 Jan)

145 The Orphan (Fox 1920) J. Gordon Edwards
     The hero fights Indians as they attack a stagecoach.
A Variety reviewer feels that producers of westerns have
come to a sad state when they "hand out film food to a

grown-up audience, consisting of a fast-riding horseman
picking off Indian braves after 'white squaws' in a stagecoach, or else on the warpath, picking them off as an
expert would demolish clay pipes in a shooting gallery."
(30 April)

146   Out of the Snows (Selznick 1920)
        In this film about life in the Canadian Northwest an
Indian woman kills a white man who slanders her. After
whites kill her in retaliation an Indian avenges her death.

147   The Third Woman (Robertson Cole 1920)
        An educated, half-breed Indian (Carlyle Blackwell)
who is struggling to decide whether to help his people
and marry among them or return to a white woman he
loves, finally chooses to live with his tribe in Arizona.

                             1921

148   Danger Valley (Independent Film Assoc. 1921)
        After a white man saves an Indian's life in a saloon
fight, the Indian shows his gratitude by leading him to
a hidden mine.

149   Flower of the North (Vitagraph 1921) David Smith
        Pierre (Joe Rickson), an loyal half-breed servant,
brings a band of friendly Indians to aid the hero.

150   Fool's Paradise (Paramount 1921) Cecil B. De Mille
        Though Indians play no significant part in this elab-
orate De Mille film, a Variety critic makes a comment
about it that reveals prejudice towards Indians on reser-
vations: "Oil did it, the same as oil made it possible for
the Injun to move a player piano into his tent, while his
fat squaw rocked herself in front and when she wanted
to smoke, removed her corncob pipe from a jeweled chate-
laine bag." (16 Dec)

151   Lonely Heart (Affiliated Dist. 1921) John O'Brien
        In the Oklahoma oil fields, Lonely Heart (Kay Laurell),
expected by her people to marry Peter Blue Fox (Escamil-
lio Fernandez), falls in love with a white man. Accused
of the murder of Blue Fox and found innocent when another Indian confesses, she finally marries the white man.

152 The Raiders (Selig 1921)
        In this film set in the Canadian Northwest, Uncas, an
     Indian guide, helps some Mounties track down whiskey
     smugglers.

153 That Girl Montana (Pathé 1921) Robert Thornby
        Montana Rivers (Blanche Sweet), who lives in an In-
     dian village under the name Tana, with her friend,
     Akkomi (Charles Edler), is finally reunited with her
     white father.

154 Western Firebrands (Aywon 1921) Charles Seeling
        Red Feather (Helen Yoder) helps the hero rescue the
     white woman. The beautiful Indian woman also provides
     some sex appeal as a Variety critic notes: "A glimpse
     of Red Feather bathing was another pretty touch." (27
     Jan 1922)

155 White Oak (Paramount 1921) Lambert Hillyer
        When the villain plots with Chief Long Knife (Chief
     Standing Bear) and the Indians attack a circled wagon
     train of pioneers, the hero comes to the rescue. At the
     end, Chief Long Knife kills the villain for betraying his
     daughter.

156 Winners of the West (Universal 1921) Edward Laemmle
        In this serial, Indians menace the heroes in chapters
     such as "Blazing Arrow."

                              1922

157 Blazing Arrows (Western Pictures 1922) Henry McCarty
        When Sky Fire (Lester Cuneo), a student at Columbia,
     falls in love with a white woman and is rejected because
     he is an Indian, he returns to the West and eventually
     rescues the same woman from the evil Gray Eagle (Clark
     Comstock). At the end he marries her when he finds out
     he is a white man who was adopted and raised by an In-
     dian.

158 Cardigan (American 1922) John Noble
        When the Indians of Chief Logan (Frank Montgomery)
     start a war, the hero is saved from being burned at the
     stake by an Indian runner. A Variety critic notes that

the "Cayuga tribe" are "costumed as the old Biograph
company presented their Indians." (24 Feb)

159   The Great Alone (American 1922) Jacques Jaccard
        Silent Duval (Monroe Salisbury), a half-breed and
      football star, leaves Stanford because of the prejudice
      toward him and returns to the Yukon where he rescues
      the one white woman who was good to him in college.
      At the end he falls in love with Nadine Picard, a patient
      half-breed.

160   The Half Breed (Assoc. First National Pics. 1922)
      Charles Taylor
        Based on the H.D. Cottrel and Oliver Morosco play,
      Half Breed: A Tale of Indian Country, this film deals
      with Delmar Spavinaw (Wheeler Oakman), an educated
      half-breed who tries to punish, in various ways, the
      judge who evicted his Indian mother from her land and
      blocked his love for a white woman.

161   The Hate Trail (Clark Cornelius Corp 1922) Milburn
      Morante
        In the Canadian Northwest, Chief Painting Cougar
      (Frank Caffray) and Moon Face (Pearl Barbour) care for
      a little white girl.

162   In the Days of Buffalo Bill (Universal 1922) Edward
      Laemmle
        In this serial, Indians threaten the hero in chapters
      like "Prisoners of the Sioux," and "The Scarlet Doom."

163   The Lonely Trail (Primex Pictures 1922)
        An Indian guide, Pierre Benorte (Fred Beauvais), res-
      cues a white woman and takes revenge on the villain who,
      years before, had seduced and deserted Pierre's sister.

164   The Man Who Paid (Producers Security Corp. 1922) Os-
      car Apfel
        Indians, one of whom is Songo (Frank Montgomery),
      aid an evil trapper in the kidnapping of a white woman
      and then kill him for double-crossing them.

165   The Mohican's Daughter (American 1922) E.V. Taylor
        Based on Jack London's "The Story of Jees Uck," this
      film deals with Jees Uck (Nancy Deaver) a half-breed

whom Chatanna (Nick Thompson), the chief of her tribe,
wants as his wife. After Chatanna kills Nashinto (Morti-
mer Snow), a medicine man, and attacks the fort, Jees
surrenders herself to him, but after the hero proves the
guilt of Chatanna, she is able to marry the hero.

166 Nanook of the North (Pathé 1922) Robert Flaherty
        This famous documentary uses an all native Eskimo
cast to show the rigors of life in the far North (for a
detailed discussion, see Brownlow, pp. 473-81).

167 One Eighth Apache (Arrow 1922) Ben Wilson
        An Apache, Charles Longdeer (Wilbur McGaugh), helps
the villain but later kills him when he finds out about
the man's crimes.

168 The Paleface (First National 1922) Buster Keaton
        Indians capture Buster Keaton and his asbestos cloth-
ing saves him from burning. They think he is a god
and take him into the tribe under the name of Little Chief
Paleface. Then he saves the tribe from being cheated by
crooked oilmen.

169 The Primitive Lover (Associated First National Pics. 1922)
Sidney Franklin
        When Big Chief Bluebottle (Chief Big Tree) treats his
wife harshly to bring her to her knees, the hero tries
to do the same with his woman.

170 The Son of the Wolf (R.C. Pictures 1922) Norman Dawn
        After a white man falls in love with Chook-Ra (Edith
Roberts), daughter of Chief Thling Tinner (Thomas
Jefferson), and rejects her for a dance hall girl, the
Chief makes her return to her people. The white man
follows her and wins her back by killing her Indian
suitor, the Bear (Fred Stanton).

171 White Eagle (Pathé 1922) W.S. Van Dyke, Fred Jackman
        In this serial, a white woman whom the Indians call
Princess White Eagle has control over some gold that dif-
ferent tribes want. Two of the chapters are "The Red
Man's Menace," and "The Flaming Arrow."

172 Winning of the West (Aywon Film Corp. 1922)
        An Indian girl, cared for by a white woman, shows

her gratitude by rescuing the woman's daughter after
Indians have kidnapped her. As the Indians are pursuing the two girls, the cavalry comes to the rescue.

173 The Woman Conquers (Assoc. First National Pics. 1922)
     Tom Forman
        In the Hudson Bay area, Lawatha (Francis McDonald),
     a faithful Indian guide, dies while trying to protect the
     heroine.

                          1923

174 The Covered Wagon (Paramount 1923) James Cruze
        Great numbers of Indians attack the wagon train.
     Tim McCoy was technical adviser for the attack sequence,
     and he used 750 Indians from various western tribes.
     Other Indian characters include Jim Bridger's two wives
     (played by Indian actresses).

175 The Huntress (Assoc. First National Pics. 1923) Lynn F.
     Reynolds
        After a white woman brought up by Indians runs away
     to avoid marrying one, a wise Indian persuades a white
     to marry her. The Indian characters are Musq'oois
     (Snitz Edwards), Beavertail (Lalo Encinas) and Otebaya
     (Chief Big Tree). A Variety reviewer comments: "The
     story deals with Indians and the old theme of the girl
     who thought she was a member of the red skin but who
     found out later that some careless parents had deserted
     her. And with the discovery that she isn't an Indian
     comes a desire to capture a white husband." (11 Oct)

176 Jamestown (Pathé 1923)
        The colonists hold Pocahontas (Dolores Cassinelli)
     hostage to force her father, Powhatan, to join them in
     fighting the Spanish. At the end, the marriage of Poca-
     hontas and John Rolfe bring the Indians and whites to-
     gether.

177 In the Days of Daniel Boone (Universal 1923) William
     Craft
        In serial chapters such as "Running the Gauntlet"
     and "Chief Blackfish Attacks," Indians threaten the hero
     as he tries to establish a colony.

178 The Santa Fe Trail (Arrow 1923) Ashton Dearholt, Robert
     Dillon
          In chapters such as "The Half Breed's Treachery,"
     "Pueblo of Death" and "The Red Menace" from this serial,
     half-breeds and Indians menace the heroes.

179 The Sting of the Scorpion (Arrow 1923) Richard Hatton
          After a cowboy befriends an Indian named Cheeko
     and rescues him from the villain, he takes the cowboy
     to a gold mine.

180 Unseeing Eyes (Goldwyn Cosmopolitan 1923) E.H. Grif-
     fith
          After Singing Pine (Frances Red Eagle) rescues the
     heroes and nurses one of them back to health, they tri-
     umph over the villain and his murderous half-breed
     companions (Paul Panzer and Dan Red Eagle) with the
     help of Eagle Blanket (Louis Deer).   ·

                              1924

181 America (UA 1924) D.W. Griffith
          In this historical drama about the revolutionary peri-
     od, Indians, two of whom are Joseph Brant (Riley Hatch),
     Chief of the Mohawks; and Hikatoo (Harry Semels), Chief
     of the Senecas, stage bloody attacks on the colonists.

182 Behind Two Guns (Sunset 1924) Robert Bradbury
          Eagle Slowfoot (William Calles) is the loyal Indian com-
     panion of the hero.

183 The Heritage of the Desert (Paramount 1924) Irvin Willat
          Mescal (Bebe Daniels), a half-breed who is rescued
     with the help of friendly Indians, ends up marrying the
     hero.

184 The Iron Horse (Fox 1924) John Ford
          In this film which deals with "the great theme of In-
     dians and soldiers" (Var., 3 Sept.), many Indians, led
     by the Cheyenne chief (Chief Big Tree) and Sioux chief
     (Chief White Spear), attack the train because they see
     the railroad as a threat to their way of life.

185 Leatherstocking (Pathé 1924) George Seitz

This serial based on Cooper's novels has chapters
such as "The Warpath," "Paleface Law," "Rivenoaks' Revenge" and "Mingo Torture."

186 Lure of the Yukon (Lee Bradford 1924) Norman Dawn
     The hero fights three Eskimos, two of whom are Black
Otter (Eagle Eye) and Kuyak (Arthur Jasmine). A
Variety critic comments on the portrayal of Kuyak:
"Jasmine's conception of an Eskimo is ... bad ... he
succeeded in projecting the illusion of a half-witted male,
nothing else." (23 July)

187 The Mine Within the Iron Door (Principal Pictures 1924)
Sam Wood
     After the hero rescues Natachee (Robert Frazer), an
educated Indian who hates whites, Natchee repays him
by not only showing the location of a gold mine but
also by killing the villain.

188 North of Nevada (Monogram 1924) Albert Rogell
     The hero brings to justice Joe Deerfoot (George Ma-
grill), an unscrupulous college-educated Indian who tries
to buy a ranch by fooling a stupid boy and kidnapping
a white woman.

189 North of 36 (Paramount 1924) Irvin Willat
     After a villain kills two Comanche women, the Indians
attack, but the hero stops the war by handing over the
villain to them for punishment.

190 Peter Pan (Paramount 1924) Herbert Brenon
     Captain Hook kidnaps the children from the Indians
who are their friends and guardians.

191 Tongues of Flame (Paramount 1924) Joseph Henabery
     When whites threaten Siwash Indians, led by Lahlett
(Bessie Love), because a judge awards them land that
had belonged to a town, the hero comes to their aid, and
not only do the Indians and whites get their rightful land
back but the hero gets Lahleet.

192 Way of a Man (Pathé 1924) George Seitz
     In this serial, the hero deals with Indians in chapters
like "Redskins and White" and "White Medicine."

1925

193 Braveheart (Producers Dist. Corp. 1925) Alan Hale
     When Braveheart (Rod La Rocque), who is an Indian
scholar and All American football player at an eastern
college, lies to protect a white friend, he has to leave
the college in disgrace with both the whites and the people
of his tribe. Later he vindicates himself by winning
fishing rights for his tribe in the courts, and by rescuing a white woman he loves after Ki-Yote (Frank Hag-
ney) has incited his tribe, one of whom is Standing Rock
(Tyrone Power), to kidnap the woman. At the end,
Braveheart gives up his love for the woman and marries
an Indian woman, Sky Arrow (Jean Acker).

194 The Gold Hunters (Davis Dist. 1925) Paul Hurst
     The hero rescues Minnetake (Hedda Nova) from the
villains and, at the end, wins her love and gets the
gold. Other Indian characters are Mukoki (Al Hallett)
and Wabigoon (Noble Johnson).

195 The Golden Strain (Fox 1925) Victor Schertzinger
     Apaches, who have been cheated out of their supplies
by a crooked Indian agent, go on the warpath.

196 Justice of the Far North (Columbia 1925) Norman Dawn
     Umluk, an Eskimo chief (Arthur Jasmine) is rescued
by a white man, and returns to his igloo to find his betrothed, Wamba (Marcia Manon) has been enticed away
by a white man. He tries to get her back but ends up
with her sister, the faithful Nootka (Laska Winter).

197 Kivalina of the Ice Lands (B.C.R. Productions 1925)
     Earl Rossman
     Aguvaluk, a hunter who is told by the witch doctor
that he must kill forty seals and a silver fox to marry
Kivalina, accomplishes the feats in this film with an all
Eskimo cast. A Variety critic comments: "In all this
the various activities of the tribe are depicted. We see
them making their boats of skin; harpooning the walrus
and the seal; skinning reindeer; constructing their igloos;
eating blubber and then making a giant wall of ice in
which to corral their herd of reindeer." (1 July)

198 The Pony Express (Paramount 1925) James Cruze

A half-breed, Charlie Bent (Frank Lackteen), leads
a band of Sioux on an attack of a town.

199 The Rainbow Trail (Fox 1925) Lynn Reynolds
     The hero stops an attack on a covered wagon and
saves an Indian woman being attacked by a half-breed.
A Variety critic notes that the film starts with a typical
pattern: "The picture starts with an Indian attack on
the wagon of a lone prospector and his family with Mix
[the hero] riding to the rescue and the routing of the
redskins." (3 June)

200 Red Love (Davis Dist. 1925) Edgar Lewis
     After Thundercloud (John Lowell), a Sioux and gradu-
ate of Carlisle, kidnaps the sheriff's half-breed daughter,
Starlight (Evangeline Russell), Little Antelope (Serrano
Keating), an Indian policeman who turns out to be his
brother, pursues and arrests him. At the end Thundercloud is exonerated and marries Starlight. Other Indian
characters are Two Crows (Frank Montgomery) and Scar-
Face (Dexter McReynolds).

201 The Red Rider (Universal 1925) Clifford Smith
     White Elk (Jack Hoxie) rejects an Indian woman he is
betrothed to for a white woman, and is condemned to
death by Chief Black Panther (Jack Pratt). He escapes,
rescues the white woman and finds out he is a white man.
Other Indian characters are Natauka (Natalie Warfield),
Silver Waters (Marin Sais), Brown Bear (Francis Ford),
the Medicine Man (Frank Lanning) and Indian chiefs
(Clark Comstock, Duke Lee and Chief Big Tree).

202 Scarlet and Gold (Davis Dist. 1925) Frank Grandon
     A Mountie marries Haida (Yvonne Pavis), who is
carrying the child of another Mountie, but she kills herself so he can marry the white woman he loves.

203 The Scarlet West (First National 1925) John Adolfi
     Cardelanche (Robert Frazer), an educated Indian re-
jected by his people, rescues the cavalry from hostile
Indians and becomes an officer in the U.S. Army. After
falling in love with a white woman and learning of the
Indians' victory over Custer, he gives up his commis-
sion and returns to his people, one of whom is Nestina
(Helen Ferguson).

204 The Thundering Herd (Paramount 1925) William Howard
       Indians surround and attack a wagon train. A Variety
     reviewer notes the film "finished with some of the best
     Indian battle stuff that has been shown in a long long
     while...." (25 Feb)

205 The Vanishing American (Paramount 1925) George Seitz
       See pages 7-9 for a discussion of this film based on
     Zane Grey's novel. A Variety critic felt the need to
     comment: "The story itself calls attention to the vanish-
     ing of the real America, the Indian, off the face of the
     North American continent. Nothing is said about the
     Indians who are living in Oklahoma at this time and draw-
     ing down a weekly royalty of about $1,750 and riding
     around in sedans which they discard immediately after
     a tire blows, so as to get a new car." (21 Oct 1925)

206 Warrior Gap (Vital 1925) Alvin J. Neitz
       Based on Charles King's Warrior Gap, A Story of the
     Sioux Outbreak of '68, this film tells of Red Cloud's
     (Len Haynes) attacks on the U.S. Cavalry.

207 The Wild Bull's Lair (Film Booking Offices 1925) Del
     Andrews
       When Indians led by Eagle Eye (Frank Hagney), an
     educated Indian who disguises himself as a white man,
     train a wild bull to lead cattle to the Indian's land, the
     hero uncovers their scheme. A Variety critic notes that
     the film "is inhabited by a tribe of Indians (not the nice,
     wild old Injuns of former days, but a group of college
     trained redskins who want to reclaim their land from the
     palefaces)." (26 Aug)

208 Wild Horse Mesa (Paramount 1925) George Seitz
       An Indian kills the villain as a revenge for the death
     of his daughter.

                              1926

209 The Big Show (Assoc. Exhibitors 1926) George Terwillinger
       Indians appear in a wild west show. A Variety critic
     refers to a comic scene in which an Indian chief in a
     "majestic pose" with "folded arms and impassive face"
     dictates a letter to his daughter which instructs "his bank

in Oklahoma to credit him with oil royalties immediately
to cover his checks drawn for a new runabout for his
daughter." (14 July)

210 Buffalo Bill on the U. P. Trail (Sunset 1926) Frank Mat-
tison
     When the chief's son, White Spear (Felix Whitefeather),
starts a buffalo stampede to cover his attack on the
whites, the hero (Roy Steward) comes to the rescue.

211 Desert Gold (Paramount 1926) George Seitz
     A Yaqui guide (Frank Lackteen) sacrifices himself in
a rockslide to save the life of the heroine.

212 The Devil Horse (Pathé 1926) Fred Jackman
     After Indians attack a wagon train, the only survivors,
the hero and a colt (the Devil Horse), both become Indian haters. After the wicked Prowling Wolf (Robert
Kortman) kidnaps a white woman he desires and incites
the Indians to attack a fort, the hero, riding the Devil
Horse (which can recognize Indians by their smell), comes
to the rescue.

213 Fighting with Buffalo Bill (Universal 1926) Ray Taylor
     Based on W. Cody's The Great West That Was, this
serial has Indians who threaten the hero in chapters entitled "The Red Menace" and "The Blazing Arrow."

214 The Flaming Frontier (Universal 1926) Edward Sedgwick
     When corrupt politicians, a crooked Indian agent and
unscrupulous buffalo hunters threaten the existence of
the Sioux, two of whom are Sitting Bull (Noble Johnson)
and Rain in the Face (Joe Bonomo), they fight back in
the Battle of Little Big Horn with Custer (Dustin Far-
num). A Variety critic notes that "the theme deals with
the swindling of the Indians out of lands by the corrupt
political Indian Ring ... that culminated in the massacre
of Custer ... and the Indian War that follows." (7
April)

215 Fort Frayne (Davis Dist. 1926) Ben Wilson
     The Indians attack the fort in reprisal for the killing
of an Indian in a saloon.

216 The Frontier Trail (Pathé 1926) Scott Dunlap

Taken prisoner by Chief Gray Wolf's (Chief Big Tree)
Sioux after making a peace offer, the hero fails to stop
an attack in which the Indians aided by a villain kill
many soldiers.

217 General Custer at Little Big Horn (Sunset 1926) Harry
Fraser
Once again, Custer (John Beck) fights the Sioux and
Cheyenne in the Battle of Little Big Horn. A Variety
critic comments: "Aside from showing as much in detail
as possible how the Indians got together for the clash
that killed Custer, it has no moral or lesson; mainly
historical, a stark tragedy of the plains, showing bodies
strewn all over 40 acres or so of land." (2 Nov 1927)

218 The Last Frontier (Producers Dist. 1926) George Seitz
Pawnee Killer (Frank Lackteen), chief of the Sioux,
attacks a wagon train, stampedes buffalo through a town
and fights with Custer.

219 War Paint (MGM 1926) W.S. Van Dyke
After Iron Eyes (Chief Yowlachie), a medicine man of
the Arapahoe whom the whites capture, escapes and attacks the fort in revenge, Chief Fearless Eagle (Chief
White Horse) helps the hero come to the rescue. A
Variety reviewer praises the writer for a script which
shows that "back in the days of the Indian extermination
all of their uprisings were not wholly the fault of the
red men." He concludes that "perhaps the moving pictures some day will tell all of the truth about the American Indian and his decline." (20 Oct)

1927

220 Arizona Nights (Film Booking Offices 1927) Lloyd Ingraham
An Indian named Red Dog (Dan Peterson) helps the
villain put pressure on a town.

221 Drums of the Desert (Paramount 1927) John Waters
After Chief Brave Bear (Bernard Siegel) and his Navajo tribe resist the villains interested in oil who try to
force them off their land and desecrate their sacred al-
tars, the cavalry stops the villains.

222 The Frontiersman (MGM 1927) Reginald Barker
        After the Creek Indians led by White Snake (Frank
     Hagney) and Grey Eagle (Chief Big Tree) massacre an
     entire fort and capture a white woman, the hero and his
     soldiers rescue the woman and stop the uprising.

223 Hawk of the Hills (Pathé 1927) Spencer Bennet
        In this serial, a savage half-breed (Frank Lackteen)
     and Indians threaten the hero in chapters like, "Doomed
     to Arrows."

224 Men of Daring (Universal 1927) Albert Rogell
        A villain incites Blackfoot, Sioux and Cheyenne led
     by Lone Wolf (Bert Apling) to attack a wagon train.

225 Open Range (Paramount 1927) Clifford Smith
        Brave Bear (Bernard Siegel), a chief bitter about
     white encroachment on his lands, joins the villain in a
     plot to steal cattle. At the end, "an old-fashioned
     Indian-cowboy battle takes place." (Var. 21 Mar 1928)

226 Policing the Plains (Canadian 1927) Arthur Kean
        Mounties deal with Sioux who have fled into Canada.
     A Variety critic notes that "a buffalo hunt ... and the
     turning back to the United States of Sitting Bull and his
     3,000 Sioux [by the Mounties] are highlights equal to
     the best in American westerns." (28 Dec)

227 Red Clay (Universal 1927) Ernst Laemmle
        Even though Chief John Nisheto (William Desmond),
     a scholar and star football player, saves the life of a
     white man in World War I, the man objects to a romance
     between John and his sister. After John is fatally shot,
     he repents his prejudice. A Variety critic comments on
     the Indian-white love theme: "It runs to the realistic,
     showing the probable results of an attempt by an Indian
     to mix with a white girl." (20 April)

228 The Red Raiders (First National Pics 1927) Albert Rogell
        Scar Face Charlie (Chief Yowlachie), an evil Indian
     spy, incites the Sioux to attack the fort, but the hero
     comes to the rescue.

229 Sitting Bull at the "Spirit Lake Massacre" (Sunset 1927)
     Robert Bradbury

This film tells the story of the famous Sioux Chief.
A <u>Variety</u> reviewer, noting that "the Indian, once the
partner of this film cowboy, has largely disappeared,"
comments that "a real Indian, Chief Yowlachie, plays
Sitting Bull and proved a better actor than any of his
white brothers." (3 Aug)

230   <u>Winners of the Wilderness</u> (MGM 1927) W.S. Van Dyke
      This film deals with the battles of the French and In-
dian War. One of the Indian characters is Pontiac (Chief
Big Tree).

                              1928

231   <u>The Glorious Trail</u> (First National Pics 1928) Albert Rogell
      Stirred up by a villain, Indians led by High Wolf
(Chief Yowlachie) attack work crews, wagon trains and
a group of settlers.

232   <u>Kit Carson</u> (Paramount 1928) Alfred L. Werker
      When Kit Carson (Fred Thomson) rescues Sing-in-the-
Clouds (Dorothy Janis), the daughter of the Blackfoot
chief, from a bear, the Indians accept him as a friend.
Later, after a villain kills Sing-in-the-Clouds, Kit re-
venges her by throwing him from a cliff into the Blackfoot "circle of death."

233   <u>Ramona</u> (UA 1928) Edwin Carewe (Chickasaw)
      In this third adaption of Helen Hunt Jackson's novel,
Ramona (Dolores Del Rio), a half-breed raised by a cruel
sheep rancher, defies her guardian by marrying Alessandro (Warner Baxter), a young Indian chief. After
she loses her husband and baby, she wanders about in
a state of amnesia until friends rescue her.

234   <u>The Riding Renegade</u> (FBO Pics 1928) Wallace Fox
      After an Indian tribe adopts the hero when he saves
the life of Little Wolf (Pedro Riga), the son of Chief
White Cloud (Nick Thompson), he and the Indians stop a
stagecoach robbery and rescue the sheriff.

235   <u>Spoilers of the West</u> (MGM 1928) W.S. Van Dyke
      After trappers and squatters on Indian land cause

trouble with the Indians of Red Cloud (Chief Big Tree),
the hero (Tim McCoy) and some Indian police stop a war.
A Variety critic comments that, "McCoy undertakes the
job supported by a handful of Indian police (a historical
detail that isn't often played up in movies or fiction).
He also notes that this film contains "spectacular Indian
fighting stuff" and that the "melodrama is dealt with in
terms of Fenimore Cooper instead of the Old Scout dime
novel style." (21 March)

236 Wyoming (MGM 1928) W.S. Van Dyke
     When Chief Big Cloud (Charles Bell), the son of Chief
Chapulti (Goes in the Lodge) and a childhood friend of
the hero, breaks a treaty by attacking the hero's wagon
train, Chief Chapulti kills his own son to stop the fighting.

<u>1929</u>

237 False Feathers (Charles Davis Prod. 1929) Horace Car-
     penter
     When Indians attack a mining town, two men drive
them away with sticks of dynamite.

238 Frozen Justice (Fox 1929) Allan Dwan
     Talu (Lenore Ulris), a half-breed Eskimo who leaves
her husband Lanak (Robert Frazer) to run away with a
wicked sea captain, returns to die in her husband's arms.

239 Hawk of the Hills (Pathé 1929) Spencer Bennet
     In this film based on the 1927 serial, Hawk (Frank
Lackteen) is a half-breed leader of a band of renegade
whites and Indians, two of which are Chief Long Hand
(Chief Yowlachie) and an Indian (Chief Whitehorse).

240 The Invaders (Syndicate Pics 1929) J.P. McGowan
     After Indians take a white girl from a wagon train,
they name her Black Fawn and she grows up with them.
Later an Indian woman reunites her with a brother who
was separated from her during the attack on the wagon
train. At the end she leaves a young warrior who loves
her.

241 Redskin (Paramount 1929) Victor Schertzinger

Wing Foot (Richard Dix), a Navajo educated in the
East and an outcast in his tribe, loves his classmate,
Corn Blossom (Gladys Belmont), who belongs to a rival
Pueblo tribe. While fleeing from her people, he discovers oil in the desert and then stops a Pueblo attack on
his village where Blossom is staying by an offer of oil
rights. Finally he marries Corn Blossom.

242 Sioux Blood (MGM 1929) John Waters
Two white brothers are separated during an Indian
uprising; one is reared by whites, the other by Indians.
The former becomes an Indian-hating scout and the latter,
who takes the name Lone Eagle (Robert Frazer), becomes
a hostile brave taught to hate whites by a medicine man
named Crazy Wolf (Chief Big Tree). Eventually the brothers recognize each other and Long Eagle leaves his tribe
to be with his brother in white society.

THE EARLY SOUND FILMS

In the silent era, films with American Indians as major characters were a popular type; in the early sound films, especially as the western took on a distinct form, Indians became more a part of the landscape, a hidden enemy, an adversary for the white hero. Though the silent films were certainly not without Indian attacks, the attack itself or the threat thereof is more notable in the early sound films. Three films epitomize this stage in the portrayal of Indians: They Died with Their Boots On, Stagecoach, and Northwest Passage. The plots of the first two turn on the threat of an Indian attack and that of the third on the journey of the whites to attack the Indians. In each case the filmmakers use the Indians as fictional adversaries to build the stature of the hero's struggles and as vehicles for cinematic excitement.

A Variety reviewer describes They Died with Their Boots On as a "surefire western, an escape from bombers, tanks and Gestapo ... American to the last man" (1941, 19 Nov). To create escapist entertainment and portray the heroes America needed during this time of war, the makers of westerns were very willing to play with history, as the same reviewer indicates: "In westerns ... major errors in history and persons, mean little to producers or audiences. The test of the yarn is not its accuracy but its speed and excitement" (1941, 19 Nov). In their attempt to mythologize Custer (Errol Flynn) into a hero who, in the Battle of Little Big Horn, sacrifices himself to insure the safety of whites in the West, the filmmakers distort the role of the Indians by diminishing them to a hidden threat or only an enemy for the attack and battle sequences.

The film follows the career of Custer from his days at West Point through the Civil War to the final battle at Little Big Horn. The first part of this film establishes Custer as a jaunty, unconventional and brave military leader--a good-natured hero whom the audience always looks up to from the

perspective of low angle shots. After Custer arrives in the
West and shapes up the Seventh Cavalry, he and his soldiers,
in the words of a printed transition in the film, "cleared the
plains for a ruthlessly spreading civilization that spelled doom
for the Red Man." The representative of the Red Men is
Crazy Horse (Anthony Quinn) and his function, like that of
all the Indians, is only to build the glory of Custer. In their
first meeting, Custer and Crazy Horse have a confrontation
on horseback in which Custer knocks Crazy Horse off his
horse. This establishes their rivalry and shows that, even
though Crazy Horse is one of the Sioux's best horsemen, he
is no match for Custer in a one-to-one fight. Later Custer
and Crazy Horse make a treaty on Indian rights to the Black
Hills and, when it is broken, Custer shows his respect for the
Sioux warrior when he says "If I were an Indian, I'd fight
with Crazy Horse until the last drop of my blood." At the
end of the battle of Little Big Horn it is Crazy Horse, the
worthy adversary, who kills Custer.

Crazy Horse is the only Indian leader that has any significant part in the film; other Indians only appear as a part
of the threatening landscape. The first images of Indians
are of Sioux lurking in the rocks waiting to ambush Custer
and his small party as they are just arriving in the West.
Later as the battle of Little Big Horn approaches, the audience sees a few long shots of Indians spying from behind
rocks, watching in trees, or hiding in the grass. Many of
these shots emphasize the vulnerability of Custer because the
camera looks down on him from the perspective of the Indians.
The only close-up view of the Indians is in a brief scene from
the Indian camp in which the leader of each tribe identifies
himself. In the actual Battle of Little Big Horn, which really
is a small part of the film, the moving camera shows the Indians closing in on Custer from every direction. They come in
waves and many die during the attack before Crazy Horse kills
Custer, who is standing above his fallen soldiers. The sense
of movement and the crosscutting between Custer and the Indians makes for a quick, exciting climax in which the audience
sees Custer as the kind of mythic hero depicted in the many
paintings of his last stand.

A more extended and classic portrayal of the Indian attack is in John Ford's Stagecoach, a film like They Died...
in which Indians gain fictional significance by their absence.
From the beginning the imagery and dialogue build suspense

about the inevitable attack of Geronimo and his Apaches with
scenes like that of the burned-out ranch with the dead white
woman, and lines such as "You're all going to be scalped and
massacred by that old butcher, Geronimo." The attack sequence itself, which comes near the end of the film, is a
classic because it both reflects and sets the patterns of film
language for such incidents. It starts from the perspective
of the Indians with an extreme high angle shot that emphasizes the vulnerability of the whites in the stagecoach. Then
the camera pans to the Apaches and stresses them as a threat
with a low angle shot of the group and then a closer shot of
Geronimo. The excitement builds with the crosscutting between the Indians and the stagecoach: an arrow out of no-
where hits a person in the stage and the chase begins with
the camera following the action at high speeds. The audience
sees whites in the stage in close shots and the Indians being
shot from their horses in longer low angle shots which emphasize how hard they are falling. Clearly the speed and action
are what are important and not the reality of the shots, as in
one when the hero shoots one bullet that knocks two Indians
off their horses at the same time. After the fast-paced editing builds the suspense to a high pitch, the sound of the
bugle signals the arrival of the cavalry and the attack is over
as quickly as it started.

    In Northwest Passage the Indians serve not as the worthy
or feared adversaries of the other two films, but as either
pathetic allies or vicious, hated enemies whose atrocities Rogers
and his Rangers must avenge. The first Indian character to
appear is drunken Konkapot, who babbles out a song as
Rogers stands above him and enlists his services as a guide.
Rogers has, at first, a good-natured disdain for this Indian.
Later, after he has massacred the Abenaki Indians, his disdain
turns nasty when he looks at the moccasins left behind and
says, "Don't any of the Redskins have man-sized feet?" and
when he refers to his victims with "There's nothing left but
roasted Indian." Rogers' Rangers show even more intense
hatred for the Indians by calling them "snakes" and "red
hellions" and telling how they scalped and burned white offi-
cers; how they tortured by tearing up the skin and prying
out ribs; or how they, along with the French, played ball
with the heads of their victims. A Ranger named Crafton
epitomizes such hatred when he hacks on an Indian with a
hatchet and then carries the head of his victim and eats from
it.

Although the Indians are described as vicious enemies, they appear in the attack scene not as strong fighters but as sheep being slaughtered. When Rogers attacks the Abenaki village in the early morning, still dazed Indians run back and forth in the center of the village as the Rangers shoot at them. Details of the massacre come out in quick cuts such as a shot from the perspective of a rifleman who leads a running Indian and shoots him like a target in a shooting gallery. Throughout the attack sequence, which is really quite short, the rapid pace of the editing and the individual shots, which are often from the perspective of the Rangers, gives the audience an exciting sense of being part of the fighting and killing of the Indians.

The cinematic excellence of the Indian fighting sequences in these films is, of course, an important part of their entertainment value as westerns. The filmmakers do not attempt to depict the Indians with any historical accuracy and show little empathy for their culture. In They Died... and Stagecoach their fictional purpose is to be a threat to the hero; in Northwest Passage, the purpose is more ominous and racist. At the end of the film, with patriotic music in the background, Rogers and the Rangers march off to the west to deal with the Plains tribes, presumably, as they did with the Abenaki. Such a connection between fighting and killing Indians and patriotism suggests that films like this might be an outlet for the hatred and fear Americans felt during and after World War II. The struggle of Rogers and other western heroes like him to conquer and punish the hated Indians parallels the efforts of American soldiers to defeat the hated Germans and Japanese. Racial hatred provides an ultimate motivation for the hero to perform his deeds, and continues to touch a chord in American audiences because Rogers is only a notable example of a long line of Indian-hating heroes in the westerns. In such films the Indians are no longer an enemy; they become the Enemy.

1930

243   The Big Trail (Fox 1930) Raoul Walsh
      Indians attack a wagon train. A Variety reviewer notes that "the silly melodrama commences to weary, for it's the same thing over and over again, including the Indian attack on the wagon train's made corral." (29 Oct)

244 The Indians Are Coming (Universal 1930) Henry MacRae
        Based on William F. Cody's The Great West That Was,
     this serial has Indians threatening the hero in chapters
     like "The Red Terror," "Circle of Death," "Redskin's
     Vengeance," and "Frontiers Aflame."

245 Santa Fe Trail (Paramount 1930) Otto Brower
        The Indians in this film are Chief Sutanek (Standing
     Bear), Eagle Feather (Blue Cloud) and Brown Beaver
     (Chief Yowlachie). A Variety critic notes that "maybe
     the Indians were cultivated in those days but here a
     couple are a takeoff of Carlisle graduates." (22 Oct)

246 The Silent Enemy (Paramount 1930) H.P. Carver
        In this fictionalized treatment of Ojibwa Indians fight-
     ing the "silent enemy" of starvation, Baluk (Chief Long
     Lance) who becomes chief after the death of Chetoga
     (Chief Yellow Robe), and survives the teachery of Dagwan
     (Chief Akawanush) the medicine man, finds a herd of
     caribou for food, and marries Neewa (Spotted Elk), the
     daughter of Chetoga. A Variety critic, referring to the
     all-Indian cast, comments that, "The characters, however,
     acted naturally. Chief Long Lance is an ideal picture
     Indian, because he is a full-blooded one, chief of his own
     tribe in these modern times, but modern himself now; an
     author of note in Indian lore, and now an actor in fact."
     (21 May)

247 Tom Sawyer (Paramount 1930) John Cromwell
        Injun Joe (Charles Stevens) is the mysterious villain
     in this version of Twain's novel.

                              1931

248 Battling with Buffalo Bill (Universal 1931) Ray Taylor
        In this serial, Buffalo Bill (Tom Tyler) and the caval-
     ry save a town from an Indian attack provoked by the
     killing of an Indian woman and the stealing of Indian
     horses. Buffalo Bill finally convinces the Indians, two of
     whom are Swift Arrow (Jim Thorpe) and Chief Thunder-
     bird (Chief Thunderbird), to accept peace and smoke
     the pipe. The serial is based on W. Cody's The Great
     West That Was and has chapters such as "Captured by
     Redskins" and "Cheyenne Vengeance."

249 The Conquering Horde (Paramount 1931) Edward Sloman
         By killing an Indian woman while she is swimming,
     the villain incites the Indians of White Cloud (Chief
     Standing Bear) to attack some cattlemen.

250 Fighting Caravans (Paramount 1931) Otto Brower and
     David Burton
         Stirred up by the villain, the Indians attack a wagon
     train. A Variety critic notes that "it's a long wait for
     the inevitable Indian attack." (1 April)

251 Great Meadow (MGM 1931) Charles Brabin
         When Indians attack a stockade and then a family of
     settlers, the father kills the Chief.

252 The Lightning Warrior (Mascot 1931) Armand Schaefer
     and Ben Kline
         In this serial, Rin-Tin-Tin, whom the Indians call the
     Lightning Warrior, helps to restore order. A villain
     known as the Wolf Man incites the Indians to attack the
     whites in chapters such as "Drums of Doom" and "Flam-
     ing Arrows."

253 Oklahoma Jim (Monogram 1931) Harry Fraser
         When a young Indian woman who had been seduced
     by a white man kills herself, the hero and a young In-
     dian (Andy Shuford) stop the hostility with her tribe by
     bringing the man to justice.

254 Red Fork Range (National Players 1931) Alvin Neitz
         Indians, one of whom is Chief Barking Fox (Chief Big
     Tree) threaten the whites on the range.

255 The Squaw Man (MGM 1931) Cecil B. De Mille
         In this third De Mille version of the E.M. Royle play,
     Naturich (Lupe Velez), daughter of Tabywana (Mitchell
     Lewis), kills herself to free her husband and son. A
     Variety reviewer feels the subject matter is out of date:
     "Indians no longer sell cattle; they own oil and many go
     to college." (22 Sept)

                              1932

256 Call Her Savage (Fox 1932) John F. Dillon

> After some wild and rebellious behavior, Nasa (Clara
> Bow), the daughter of a white woman and an Indian
> named Moonglow (Gilbert Roland), finds out about her
> identity and falls in love with a young half-breed.

257 End of the Trail (Columbia 1932) R. Lederman
The hero (Tim McCoy), the beloved of Luana (Luana
Walters) gives up his rank and position in the army to
try to bring peace between the Indians of Chief Red
Cloud (Chief White Eagle) and the whites. Throughout
the film he makes statements about the unfair treatment
of Indians, such as, "We've never kept a single treaty
with them. That's why I'm for the Indians, because in
every instance the white man has been to blame." (Tuska
252)

258 Heroes of the West (Universal 1932) Ray Taylor
In this serial, with chapters entitled "The Red Peril"
and "Captured by Indians," Indians, two of whom are
Buckskin Joe (Frank Lackteen) and Thunderbird (Chief
Thunderbird), threaten the hero who is trying to build
one part of the transcontinental railroad.

259 Igloo (Universal 1932) Ewing Scott
After Chee-ak, an Eskimo hunter from another tribe,
marries Kyatuk, the daughter of the Chief, he leads her
tribe of Eskimos on an arduous trip to the sea during
the winter. Despite a revolt along the way, they finally
make it to the sea and find food. A Variety critic explains that the film is: "... a new epic of the north
bearing the authentic stamp of Arctic rigors and played
with utmost gravity by a whole Eskimo village, led by a
native giant Chee-ak." (26 July)

260 Last of the Mohicans (Mascot 1932) Reeves Eason, Ford
Beebe
In this serial, the first chapter shows the Mohicans
being massacred, and the last shows Chingachgook (Hobart Bosworth) killing Magua (Robert Kortman). Hawkeye (Harry Carey) and Uncas (Junior Coughlin) appear
in chapters such as "A Redskin's Honor" and "Paleface
Magic."

261 Rainbow Trail (Fox 1932) David Howard
Indians, one of whom is Lone Eagle (Robert Frazer),

threaten a wagon train to provide, in the words of a
Variety critic, "some Indian menace stuff." (2 Feb)

262 Texas Pioneers (Monogram 1932) Harry Fraser
        Using guns sold to them by a villain, Indians (two of
     whom are played by Chief Standing Bear and Iron Eyes
     Cody) attack a fort.

263 White Eagle (Columbia 1932) Lambert Hillyer
        White Eagle (Buck Jones), a pony express rider, joins
     his father Grey Wolf (Frank Campeau) to bring to justice
     villains disguised as Indians who have caused hostility
     between the whites and Indians. A New York Times
     critic comments that in films like this "the pony express,
     horse thieves ... Indians, stagecoach robbers and the
     men in governmental blue produced the heroes and scamps
     that have thrilled big and little boys ever since." (24
     Sept 18)

                              1933

264 Clancy of the Mounted (Universal 1933) Ray Taylor
        In this serial, renegade half-breeds threaten the hero
     and heroine in the chapter called "The Breed Strikes."

265 Eskimo (MGM 1933) W.S. Van Dyke
        This film adapted from the books of Peter Freuchen
     has an all-native cast and deals with the differences be-
     tween Eskimo and white justice when the Mounties come
     after the head man, Mala, who has committed a rape.

266 Fighting with Kit Carson (Mascot 1933) Armand Schaefer
     and Colbert Clark
        In this serial, Kit Carson (Johnny Mack Brown) and
     his faithful Indian friend Nakomas (Noah Beery, Jr.) are
     the heroes in chapters such as "The White Chief" and
     "Red Phantoms."

267 King of the Wild Horses (Columbia 1933) Earl Haley
        Navajos, two of whom are Red Wolf (William Janney)
     and Wanima (Dorothy Appleby), appear in a film a Vari-
     ety reviewer describes as "a Navajo scene with yards and
     yards of unimportant tribal ceremonies to still more yards
     of horses running and fighting." (27 Mar)

268 SOS Iceberg (Universal 1933) Tony Garnett
     Eskimos in kayaks rescue the main character.

269 The Telegraph Trail (Vitagraph 1933) Tenny Wright
     The Indians, urged on by the villain, attack the camp
of the telegraph workers. A Variety critic comments:
"This outline has been used before: the white man uses
his Indian allies to check the march of progress." (4
April)

270 The Thundering Herd (Paramount 1933) Henry Hathaway
     Indians attack buffalo hunters who are slaughtering
their herds.

                              1934

271 Laughing Boy (MGM 1934) W.S. Van Dyke
     Based on the novel Laughing Boy by Oliver Lafarge,
this film tells of the tragic love between Slim Girl (Lupe
Velez), an Indian prostitute who deals with white men,
and Laughing Boy (Ramon Novarro), a young Navajo.
After Slim Girl and Laughing Boy are married, she plays
her white lover against her husband and vice versa.
Finally, Laughing Boy finds her in the house near the
railroad tracks where she meets her white lovers, and he
kills her with an arrow intended for the white man she
is with. Other Indian characters are Laughing Boy's
father (Chief Thunder Cloud), mother (Catalina Rambala),
Wounded Face (Tall Man's Boy), Yellow Singer (F.A. Ar-
ments), Squaw's Son (Deer Spring) and Red Man (Pelli-
cana). A Variety critic notes that the film uses these
"McCoy Indians as atmosphere, some of whom speak flaw-
less English." (15 May)

272 Massacre (First National 1934) Alan Crosland
     In this film based on the Robert Gessner novel, Joe
Thunder Horse (Richard Barthelmess), a college-educated
Sioux who rides in a wild west show and flirts with white
women, is called home by his father, the chief, to help
the tribe fight the villains who are exploiting them on
the reservation. In Washington, Joe wins back the rights
of his people and ends up marrying an educated Indian
woman (Ann Dvorak). A Variety critic comments on the
white actor Barthelmess, "Worst of all, when surrounded

by other big chiefs who are Indians on the up and up,
he doesn't look an Indian any more than Jimmy Durante
looks like a Chinaman." (23 Jan)

273 Wagon Wheels (Paramount 1934) Charles Barton
     In this version of the 1931 Fighting Caravans, Indians,
spurred on by a villain, attack a wagon train.

274 Wheels of Destiny (Universal 1934) Alan James
     The Indians, one of whom is Scalp-em-Alive (Fred
Sale, Jr.), attack wagon trains in a film that a Variety
critic says has a lot of "shooting, shouting, and Indian
whooping." (3 April)

                              1935

275 Annie Oakley (RKO 1935) George Stevens
     The heroine performs in Buffalo Bill's (Moroni Olsen)
Wild West Show along with her friend Sitting Bull (Chief
Thunder Cloud) and his Sioux Indians. A Variety critic
comments, "A large group of Indians give it both color
and comedy.... Audiences will find something different
and highly amusing in the antics of Chief Thunder Cloud,
impersonating the famous Sitting Bull." (25 Dec)

276 Behold My Wife (Paramount 1935) Mitchell Leisen
     Based on Translation of a Savage by Sir Gilbert Parker,
the film tells the story of Tonita Stormcloud (Sylvia Sidney), the daughter of a chief, who saves the life of a
white man who, in turn, marries her to get back at his
family. When Tonita realizes her husband's motive, she
tries to revenge herself, but they are eventually recon-
ciled. Other Indian characters are a medicine man (Greg
Whitespear) and the Indian chief (Jim Thorpe).

277 Fighting Pioneers (Resolute 1935) Harry Fraser
     After her father, the chief dies, Wa-Na-Na (Ruth Mix)
leads her tribe against the soldiers. At the end, she
falls in love with the hero.

278 The Miracle Rider (Mascot 1935) Armand Schaefer and
     Reeves Eason
     In this serial, Chapter 1 called "The Vanishing Indian,"
gives a long history of American heroes who have helped

Indians when they are threatened by villains. The hero
(Tom Mix), adopted into the Ravenhead tribe led by Chief
Black Wing (Robert Frazer) and helped by his daughter
Ruth (Jean Gale), triumphs over the villains who are
aided by a bad Indian, Longboat (Robert Kortman). In
gratitude the Indians, two of whom are Chief Two Hawks
(Black Hawk) and Chief Last Elk (Chief Standing Bear),
send the hero and Ruth to Washington as their representatives.

279   Rustlers of Red Dog (Universal 1935) Louis Frielander
      In this serial, with chapters like "Hostile Indians" and
"Flaming Arrow," Indians threaten the whites with attacks on a wagon train, fort and stagecoach. After the
Indians take prisoners, the hero rescues men about to
be burned to death and the heroine, who is being forced
to marry an Indian. Chief Thunder Cloud, Chief Thunderbird and Jim Thorpe play some of the Indians.

280   Western Frontier (Columbia 1935) Albert Herman
      Indians kill everyone in a family heading west in a
covered wagon except the young girl whom they kidnap.

                              1936

281   Custer's Last Stand (Stage and Screen 1936) Elmer Clif-
ton
      In this serial, in chapters such as "Warpath" and "Red
Panthers," Young Wolf and the Dakotas attack settlers
and then, with the villain called Keen Blade, threaten the
hero. Chief Thunder Cloud, Chief Big Tree, Iron Eyes
Cody and High Eagle play Indians.

282   Daniel Boone (RKO 1936) David Howard
      Led by a gun-selling villain, Indians attack Boone's
(George O'Brien) settlement and are about to win when
rain washes out their underground tunnels. A Variety
critic notes that the film uses "a lot of phoney histrionics
and make-believe hysterical Indian fighting.... It's an
Indian opera à la mode." (28 Oct)

283   Desert Gold (Paramount 1936) James Hogan
      In this film based on the Zane Grey novel, the hero
helps Moya (Buster Crabbe) and his tribe survive the attack of villains after their gold.

284 The Glory Trail (Crescent 1936) Lynn Shores
     Indians attack whites who are building a road across
the West, in a film a Variety critic describes as "a fair
action thriller of the gunpowder and Injun brand ...
with beaucoup scraps between the Indians and paleface."
(21 April)

285 Last of the Mohicans (UA 1936) George Seitz
     In this version of Cooper's novel, both Hawkeye
(Randolph Scott) and Uncas (Phillip Reed) fall in love
and, when Magua (Bruce Cabot) knocks Uncas off a cliff,
Uncas' white lover also jumps. Then Chingachgook
(Robert Barrat) kills Magua, and Hawkeye goes to his
woman. A NYT critic comments: "The massacre of Fort
William Henry is by far the bloodiest, scalpingest morsel
of cinematic imagery ever produced, and we were conse-
quently about ready to overlook the elisions made neces-
sary in fitting the novel to the screen when Hollywood
permitted Hawkeye to fall in love." (3 Sept 17)

286 The Phantom Rider (Universal 1936) Ray Taylor
     In this serial, in chapters such as "The Indian Raid,"
Indians menace whites.

287 The Plainsman (Paramount 1936) Cecil B. De Mille
     Wild Bill Hickok (Gary Cooper), Buffalo Bill (James
Ellison), and Custer (John Miljan) battle Comanches led
by Yellow Hand (Paul Harvey) and Painted Horse (Victor
Varconi). A Variety critic notes that the film deals with
"cowboys and Indians on a broad sweeping scale ..."
and that "The spec appeal is in the redskin warfare."·
(20 Jan 1937)

288 Ramona (20th Cent-Fox 1936) Henry King
     In this version of Helen H. Jackson's novel, Ramona
(Loretta Young) and Alessandro (Don Ameche) suffer at
the hands of prejudiced whites. Though more recent
critics have found the film to be poorly cast, a Variety
critic notes that "Loretta Young, in a coal black wig, is
a lovely Indian girl and the color adds to her attractive-
ness." (14 Oct)

289 Ride, Ranger, Ride (Republic 1936) Joseph Kane
     When the Comanches, one of whom is Little Wolf (Chief
Thunder Cloud), aided by Tavibo (Monte Blue), an Indian

interpreter for an army post, attack a wagon train, Gene
Autrey and the Texas Rangers come to the rescue.

290 Rose Marie (MGM 1936) W.S. Van Dyke
     In this famous musical, Indians in stylized costumes
     appear in the lavish production of "Totem Tom Tom."
     Also the popular "Indian Love Call" reflects the Indian
     motif.

291 The Texas Rangers (Paramount 1936) King Vidor
     Indians attack a farmhouse and then do battle with
     the hero and the Rangers by throwing large stones from
     a mountain top.

292 Treachery Rides the Range (Warner 1936) Frank McDonald
     After an evil band of buffalo hunters break a treaty,
     the Indians, among whom are Little Big Wolf (Carlyle
     Moore), Chief Red Smoke (Jim Thorpe), Little Big Fox
     (Frank Bruno) and Antelope Boy (Dick Botiller), attack
     the whites.

293 Tundra (Burrough-Tarzan 1936) Norman Dawn
     In this Eskimo film in the "general classification of
     wild animal-native actor group," (Var. 9 Dec) the hero
     helps sick Eskimos and fights various arctic animals.

294 West of Nevada (First Division 1936) Robert Hill
     Villains try to steal gold from some good Indians,
     one of whom is Bald Eagle (Dick Botiller). A Variety
     critic notes that "juvenile audiences will thrill to see
     that redskins are once again in favor with the Hollywood
     chiefs." (22 July)

                              1937

295 Hills of Old Wyoming (Paramount 1937) Nate Watt
     After the villain, a lawman on a reservation who has
     half-breeds rustle cattle for him, causes trouble between
     the Indians and the cattlemen, Hopalong Cassidy saves
     the day.

296 The Outcasts of Poker Flat (RKO 1937) Christy Cabanne
     Indian Jim (Monte Blue) is one of the villains in this
     film based on the Bret Harte story.

297 The Painted Stallion (Republic 1937) William Witney, Ray
     Taylor
         In this serial, villains incite the Indians to attack a
     wagon train. A young Indian woman who rides the
     painted stallion warns the whites of the danger by shoot-
     ing whistling arrows in a chapter called "The Whispering
     Arrow." The rider (Julia Thayer), who is really a white
     woman, is worshipped as a goddess by the Comanches
     because of her blonde hair.

298 Prairie Thunder (Warner 1937) Reeves Eason
         Supplied with guns by the villain, the Indians attack
     a construction camp and town of railroad and telegraph
     builders. A Variety critic notes: "The plot is reminis-
     cent of past Indian epics and carries stock shots of war
     dances, etc. from them ... ace high with the juves."
     (1 Dec)

299 Riders of the Whistling Skull (Republic 1937) Mack Wright
         Indians, two of whom are Otah (Yakima Canutt) and
     the High Priest (Chief Thunder Cloud), threaten the
     three Mesquiteers as they search for the lost Indian city
     of Lukachaki.

300 Wells Fargo (Paramount 1937) Frank Lloyd
         Indians attack the stagecoaches of this company.

301 Wild West Days (Universal 1937) Ford Beebe, Cliff Smith
         In this serial, with chapters like "The Redskins Re-
     venge," "The Indians are Coming," and "Rustlers and
     Redskins," Red Hatchet (Chief Thunderbird) and his
     tribe threaten the heroes.

                              1938

302 Flaming Frontiers (Universal 1938) Ray Taylor, Alan
     James
         In this serial, in chapters like "The Savage Horde,"
     "Half Breeds Revenge," and "The Indians are Coming,"
     Indians, one of whom is Thunder Cloud (Chief Thunder
     Cloud), menace Buffalo Bill (John Rutherford) and the
     heroine.

303 The Great Adventures of Wild Bill Hickok (Columbia 1938)
     Mack Wright, Sam Nelson

In chapters of this serial like "The Apache Killer" and "Savage Vengeance," Indians, such as Grey Eagle (Chief Thunder Cloud), Little Elk (Ray Mala) and Snake Eyes (Roscoe Ates), threaten the hero.

304 Hawk of the Wilderness (Republic 1938) William Witney, John English
       In this serial, Mokuyi (Noble Johnson) is the faithful Indian companion of the hero, Kioga, who had been raised by Indians who live on an island. A friendly Indian woman, Kias (Mala), rescues white prisoners and eventually gives her life to save the hero. Yellow Weasel (Monte Blue) is an evil witch doctor.

305 The Lone Ranger (Republic 1938) William Witney, John English
       This serial marks the first appearance of this hero and his faithful companion, Tonto (Chief Thunder Cloud), who appears in a chapter called "Red Man's Courage."

306 Overland Express (Columbia 1938) Drew Eberson
       Indians and stagecoach line owners threaten the founders of the Pony Express. A Variety critic notes that "a couple of Injuns on warpath sequences drag in library clips that don't jive with groups [of Indians] actually in the production." (11 May)

307 The Texans (Paramount 1938) James Hogan
       Indians attack cowboys on a cattle drive.

308 Tom Sawyer (UA 1938) Norman Taurog
       Commenting on this version of Twain's novel, a Variety critic notes that "Injun Joe is played by Victor Jory with all the fiendish villainy in the part." (16 Feb)

309 Where the Buffalo Roam (Monogram 1938) Al Herman
       The hero brings to justice villains who have been killing buffalo contrary to the treaty guaranteeing these animals as food for the Indians.

1939

310 Across the Plains (Monogram 1939) Spencer Bennet
       Cherokee (Frank Randall), a white man raised by that

tribe, and his Indian friends rescue his long-lost brother
from a gang of villains.

311 Allegheny Uprising (RKO 1939) William Seiter
        Supplied with liquor and guns by the villains, Indians
attack the settlers.

312 Bad Lands (RKO 1939) Lew Landers
        Apaches pick off a pursuing posse one by one until
soldiers save the last survivor.

313 Drums Along the Mohawk (20th Cent-Fox 1939) John Ford
        In this revolutionary period drama, Blue Back (Chief
Big Tree) is a Christian Indian with a sense of humor
and the loyal companion of the white hero. The Iroquois,
led by a Tory, are bloodthirsty enemies who burn farms
and attack a fort.

314 The Lone Ranger Rides Again (Republic 1939) William
Witney
        In this serial, the hero and Tonto (Chief Thunder
Cloud) protect a wagon train of settlers.

315 The Oregon Trail (Universal 1939) Ford Beebe
        In chapters from this serial like "Indian Vengeance"
and "Redskin Revenge," a villain incites the Indians to
attack wagon trains.

316 Overland with Kit Carson (Columbia 1939) Sam Nelson,
Norman Deming
        In this serial, described as "a lame script western
filled with Indians, renegades and gun runners," (Var.
11 Oct) Indians threaten the hero (Bill Elliot).

317 Scouts to the Rescue (Universal 1939) Ray Taylor, Allan
James
        The Indians here reach a low point; their attack is
stopped by a group of Boy Scouts.

318 Stagecoach (UA 1939) John Ford
        Geronimo (Chief White Horse), informed by Yakeema
(Elvira Rios), the Indian wife of a Mexican, attacks a
stagecoach. An Indian scout, who appears at the beginning, is played by Chief Big Tree. See pages 51-54 for
further discussion.

319   Susannah of the Mounties (20th Cent-Fox 1939) William
      Seiter
          Blackfoot, three of whom are Little Chief (Martin Good
      Rider), Chief Big Eagle (Maurice Moscovich) and Wolf
      Pelt (Victory Jory), raid a railroad construction camp
      and the Mounties' post. A Variety critic comments:
      "Capturing Randolph Scott for a burning-at-the-stake
      party, the Indians are persuaded to smoke a pipe of
      peace when Shirley [Temple] goes to the redskins' camp
      and explains all to the understanding chief." (21 June)

320   Union Pacific (Paramount 1939) Cecil B. De Mille
          Indians threaten the heroes and disrupt the building
      of the railroad by derailing and looting the train.

321   Wolf Call (Monogram 1939) George Waggner
          The hero falls in love with Towanah (Movita), an In-
      dian woman.

322   Zorro's Fighting Legion (Republic 1939) William Witney,
      John English
          A villain tricks superstitious Yaqui Indians, and Juan
      (Budd Buster) is a faithful Indian servant in this serial.

                              1940

323   Adventures of Red Ryder (Republic 1940) William Witney,
      John English
          In this serial, the hero has a young Indian companion,
      Little Beaver (Tommy Cook).

324   Arizona (Columbia 1940) Wesley Ruggles
          Apaches attack a wagon train and cowboys on a cattle
      drive.

325   Geronimo (Paramount 1940) Paul Sloane
          In this film described as "a fast moving tale of lusty
      Indian fighting" (Var. 22 Nov 1939), Geronimo (Chief
      Thunder Cloud), who is supplied with guns and ammuni-
      tion by a villain, proves to be a fierce enemy of the
      whites.

326   Hi-Yo Silver (Republic 1940) William Witney
          This film, put together from the 1939 serial, features
      Chief Thunder Cloud as Tonto.

327 Kit Carson (UA 1940) George Seitz
       The hero (Jon Hall) battles Shoshone Indians.

328 My Little Chickadee (Universal 1940) Edward Kline
       In this comedy, Mae West skillfully picks off Indians
attacking the train she is riding on, and W.C. Fields
has an educated Indian friend named Milton, who just
grunts.

329 North West Mounted Police (Paramount 1940) Cecil B.
De Mille
       This film deals with the revolt of Louis Riel (Francis
McDonald), the leader of half-breeds called Metis. Lou-
vette Corbeau (Paulette Goddard), a half-breed femme
fatale, entices a Mountie who loves her to leave his post
and thus allow an ambush. The wise Indian leader is
Chief Big Bear (Walter Hampden), and other Indians are
played by Ray Mala, Monte Blue, Chief Yowlachie, Chief
Thunderbird and Chief Thunder Cloud.

330 Northwest Passage (MGM 1940) King Vidor
       The heroes attack an Abenaki village in this film
based on part of Kenneth Robert's novel. See pages
51-54 for further discussion.

331 Pony Post (Universal 1940) Ray Taylor
       Indians threaten the hero in "a couple of sequences
with some tired Indian warriors on the loose." (Var.
25 Dec)

332 Prairie Schooners (Columbia 1940) Sam Nelson
       Wild Bill Hickok (Bill Elliot) fights Indians led by
Chief Sanche (Jim Thorpe). A Variety critic comments:
"The plot does the redskins dirt, maybe the Indians en-
camped in Colorado at the time were that dumb but it
hardly is conceivable.... Another quaint twist is the
failure of the Indians to come out victorious although
outnumbering the white settlers about two to one." (13
Nov)

333 Winners of the West (Universal 1940) Ford Beebe, Ray
Taylor
       In this serial, in chapters such as, "Trapped by Red-
skins," "Sacrificed by Savages," and "The Battle of Black-
hawk," an evil half-breed, Snakeye (Charles Stevens),

Jay Silverheels as Tonto in <u>The Lone Ranger</u>

PRINCESS REDWING IN....

"AS TOLD BY PRINCESS BESS"

ANOTHER SELIG HIT

K·A·L·E·M KLM PICTURES presents

Princess **Mona Darkfeather** with EDWIN AUGUST......

......in **The CRY of the LOON**

The Battle of Elderbush Gulch (1913)

Iron Eyes Cody

Charles Stevens as Injun Joe in Tom Sawyer (1930)

Jay Silverheels

Top: <u>War Paint</u> (1926)
Bottom: Chief Thunder Cloud in <u>Hi-Yo Silver</u> (1940)
Opposite: Indian actors play Navajos in <u>Wagonmaster</u> (1950)

Above:　An Indian actor in <u>Tale of the Navajos</u> (1949)

Opposite:　Indian Warrior in <u>Pony Soldier</u> (1952)

Top: Chief Yowlachie in Son of Geronimo (1960)
Bottom: The hero of The Savage (1952) (Charlton Heston)
surrounded by Indian actors
Opposite: Indian encampment in Pawnee (1957)

An Indian attack in Davy Crockett—King of the Wild Frontier (1955)

Top: Chief Yowlachie in <u>Son of Geronimo</u> (1960)
Bottom: The hero of <u>The Savage</u> (1952) (Charlton Heston)
surrounded by Indian actors
Opposite: Indian encampment in <u>Pawnee</u> (1957)

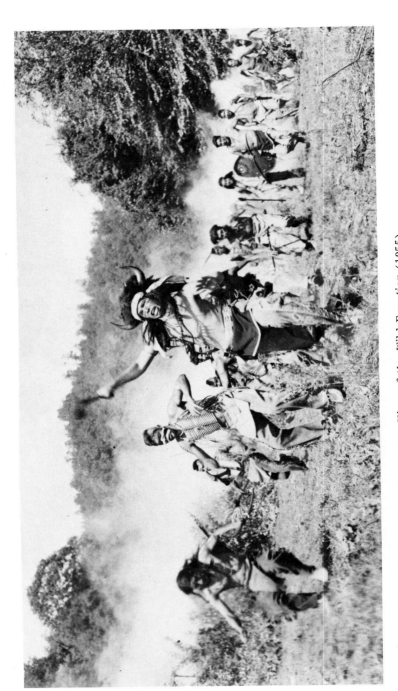

An Indian attack in <u>Davy Crockett--King of the Wild Frontier</u> (1955)

Indian actors in Apache Chief (1949)

Top: Chief Dan George (left) in <u>Little Big Man</u> (1970)
Bottom: Will Sampson (right) in <u>The White Buffalo</u> (1977)

tries to stop the building of the railroad by leading the
Indians on raids against construction camps, stagecoaches,
wagon trains and telegraph stations. Eventually, Chief
War Eagle (Chief Yowlachie), signs a peace treaty.

334 Wyoming (MGM 1940) Richard Thorpe
       Threatening Indians prompt a Variety critic to com-
ment, "Scripters inject pyrotechnics of an Indian attack
on the ranches for an old fashioned battle a la Elderbush
Gulch (early D.W. Griffith)." (11 Sept)

335 Young Buffalo Bill (Republic 1940) Joseph Kane
       Roy Rogers has to deal with an Indian attack led by
Akuna (Chief Thunder Cloud).

1941

336 Badlands of Dakota (Universal 1941) Alfred E. Green
       Sioux make a night attack on a village.

337 Hudson's Bay (20th Cent-Fox 1941) Irving Pichel
       Indians threaten to make war with the traders.

338 The Pioneers (Monogram 1941) Al Herman
       In this film based on the Cooper novel, villains intent
on laying claim to a rich valley incite Indians, two of
whom are Warcloud (Chief Many Treaties) and Lonedeer
(Chief Soldani), to attack a wagon train to stop it from
getting to the valley.

339 Thunder over the Prairie (Columbia 1941) Lambert Hillyer
       When an Indian medic gets in trouble for revealing
that a construction company mistreats its Indian workers,
the hero comes to his rescue and proves he has been
framed by the villain.

340 Western Union (20th Cent-Fox 1941) Fritz Lang
       The Indians, two of whom are Chief Spotted Horse
(Chief Big Tree) and an Indian leader (Chief Thunder
Cloud) threaten the hero (Dean Jagger). A Variety
critic comments, "The Indians, real ones from the reserva-
tions, act normally at all times, and although antagonistic
at first to the stretching of wires across their reservation, are finally won over by Jagger without a battle."
(5 Feb)

341 White Eagle (Columbia 1941) James Horne
        In this serial (a remake of the 1932 film), White Eagle
     (Buck Jones), a pony express rider, joins his father,
     Grey Wolf, in a war on the whites after the villains dis-
     guised as Indians give his people a bad name. Eventually,
     the Indians, one of whom is Running Deer (Chief Yow-
     lachie), capture the villains, and White Eagle gets the
     white girl.

                              1942

342 Lawless Plainsmen (Columbia 1942) William Berke
        Indians, two of whom are Tascosa (Stanley Brown)
     and Ochella (Nick Thompson), attack a wagon train. A
     Variety critic comments that the "story's a standard one
     of the unscrupulous white man making a deal with Indians
     to attack a wagon train." (10 June)

343 The Omaha Trail (MGM 1942)
        Indians attack a wagon train.

344 Overland Mail (Universal 1942) Ford Beebe, John Rawlins
        In this serial, Indians and villains disguised as In-
     dians threaten the heroes. Chief Thunder Cloud and
     Chief Many Treaties play two of the Indians.

345 Perils of the Royal Mounted (Columbia 1942) James Horne
        In this serial, with such chapter titles as "Burned at
     the Stake," Indians led by Black Bear (Nick Thompson),
     an evil medicine man who conspires with the villain, are
     a menace to the whites. Other Indian characters are
     Flying Cloud (Art Miles) and Little Wolf (Richard Vallin).

346 Ride 'Em Cowboy (Universal 1942) Arthur Lubin
        In this Abbott and Costello comedy, originally titled
     No Indians Please, Jack Rainwater (Douglass Dumbrille)
     is an Indian who threatens the comic heroes.

347 Ten Gentlemen from West Point (20th Cent-Fox 1942)
     Henry Hathaway
        New cadets, using a strategy they just learned in
     the classroom, stop a Shawnee uprising led by Tecumseh
     (Noble Johnson).

348 **They Died with Their Boots On** (Warner 1942) Raoul
Walsh
     This film deals with George A. Custer from his days
at West Point to the Battle of Little Big Horn. See pages
51-54 for further discussion.

349 **Valley of the Sun** (RKO 1942) George Marshall
     The Apaches led by Geronimo (Tom Tyler) and Co-
chise (Antonio Moreno) attack the whites. A *Variety*
reviewer notes that "it's the time worn tale of a young
frontiersman and friend of the Indians who tangles with
the civilian administrator, whose treatment of the Indians
sets them on the warpath." (14 Jan)

                          1943

350 **Apache Trail** (MGM 1943) Richard Thorpe
     Apaches threaten white settlers. A *Variety* reviewer
comments: "Of course, the film's major detail, the uprising of the Apaches against the whites, is something
that's long since seen its best picture days, but the
youngsters should find it fairly diverting entertainment
nevertheless." (24 June)

351 **Daredevils of the West** (Republic 1943) John English
     In this serial, Indians, led by a chief played by Chief
Thunder Cloud, attack in a chapter called "Redskin
Raiders."

352 **Deerslayer** (Republic 1943) Lew Landers
     In this adaptation of Cooper's novel, the hero (Bruce
Kellogg) aided by the Delaware struggles with the hostile Huron who attack a fort and a riverboat. The Indian
characters are Wah 'Tah (Yvonne De Carlo), Chief Riven-
oak (Trevor Bardette), Chief Uncas (Robert Warwick),
Chief Brave Eagle (Chief Many Treaties), Duenna (Princess
Whynemak) and the Huron sub-chief (William Edmund).
A *Variety* critic comments: "Deerslayer is a super-hero,
who continuously eludes the Indians, and, when he's
captured, easily escapes at the most convenient spots for
script purposes." (10 Nov)

353 **Frontier Fury** (Columbia 1943) William Berke
     The villains steal from the hero supplies meant for the

Indians, two of whom are Chief Eagle Feather (Billy
Wilkerson) and Gray Bear (Stanley Brown). He finally
gets the supplies back and saves the Indians from a winter without food.

354 The Law Rides Again (Monogram 1943) Alan James
        The heroes bring to justice a crooked Indian agent
     and his men who are starting trouble with the Indians,
     three of whom are Eagle Eye (Emmett Lynn), Barking
     Fox (Chief Many Treaties) and one played by Chief Thun-
     der Cloud.

355 Wagon Tracks West (Republic 1943) Howard Bretherton
        The heroes help Fleetwing (Rick Vallin), an Indian
     doctor in love with Moonbush (Anne Jeffreys), to handle
     a corrupt Indian agent and Clawtooth (Tom Tyler), a
     wicked medicine man. A Variety critic comments: "The
     Femme lead could have been handled by a totem pole
     wired for sound. Anne Jeffreys, as the Indian maid,
     doesn't even get a chance to smile, has very few lines,
     and is completely eliminated from the story" [by the end
     of the film]. (27 Oct)

356 Wild Horse Stampede (Monogram 1943) Alan James
        A band of horse rustlers incite the Indians to attack
     whites who are building a railroad through the Southwest.

                              1944

357 Black Arrow (Columbia 1944) Lew Landers
        In chapters of this serial such as "An Indian's Re-
     venge" and "Black Arrow Triumphs," Black Arrow
     (Robert Scott), the son of Aranho, the Navajo chief,
     who later finds out he is a white man, triumphs over the
     Indian villain, Snake-That-Walks (George Lewis), with
     the help of the heroine.

358 Buffalo Bill (20th Cent-Fox 1944) William Wellman
        Buffalo Bill (Joe McCrea) has a hand-to-hand battle
     to the death with his former friend, Yellow Hand (Anthony
     Quinn), which allows the cavalry to come to the rescue
     in a large Indian battle. Other Indian characters are
     Tall Bull (Chief Many Treaties), Crazy Horse (Chief
     Thunder Cloud), a medicine man (Nick Thompson), an

old Indian woman (Talzumbia Dupes) and Dawn Starlight
(Linda Darnell) an Indian school teacher who loves the
hero.

359 Outlaw Trail (Monogram 1944) Robert Tansey
     Thundercloud (Chief Thunder Cloud) is an Indian who
becomes one of the Trail Blazers (Hoot Gibson, Bob
Steele) and shares in their exploits. This character also
appears in Sonora Stagecoach, another 1944 Monogram
Trail Blazers film.

                              1945

360 Dakota (Republic 1945) Joseph Kane
     Indians are blamed for burning out homesteaders even
though it is the work of the villain.

361 The Man from Oklahoma (Republic 1945) Frank McDonald
     During the settling of the Oklahoma Territory, Roy
Rogers deals with Indians, two of whom are Chief Red
Feather (Charles Soldani) and Little Bird on the Wing
(June Bryde).

362 Navajo Kid (PRC 1945) Harry Fraser
     The Navajo Kid, a white man adopted by the Indians,
takes vengeance on the killer of his Indian foster father.

                              1946

363 Bad Bascomb (MGM 1946) Sylvan Simon
     Indians attack a Mormon wagon train and, in what may
be the ultimate put-down of Indian fighting ability, a
girl fends them off with a pea shooter.

364 Canyon Passage (Universal 1946) Jacques Tourneur
     In Oregon, Indians (whose spokesman is played by
Chief Yowlachie) attack settlers and set fire to their
cabins.

365 Duel in the Sun (Selznick 1946) King Vidor
     Pearl Chavez (Jennifer Jones) is a young half-breed
whom two brothers desire. A victim of prejudice and her
own passionate nature, she dies, like her Indian mother,
in the arms of her lover.

366 My Darling Clementine (20th Cent-Fox 1946) John Ford
        At the beginning of the film the drunken Indian Joe
     (Charles Stevens) terrorizes the town until Wyatt Earp
     stops him.

367 The Phantom Rider (Republic 1946) Spencer Bennet,
     Fred Brannon
        In this serial, Indians, two of whom are Blue Feather
     (George Lewis) and Yellow Wolf (Chief Thunder Cloud),
     are characters in chapters such as "The Captive Chief."

368 Romance of the West (PRC 1946) Robert Emmett
        Villains intent on getting some land rich with silver
     try to provoke the Indians led by Chief Eagle Feather
     (Chief Thunder Cloud), but a good Indian agent stops
     the war.

369 The Scarlet Horseman (Universal 1946) Ray Taylor, Lewis
     Collins
        In chapters from this serial such as "Comanche Ava-
     lanche" and "Staked Plains Massacre," the hero, who
     takes on the identity of the Scarlet Horseman, a legendary
     hero of the Comanches, deals with Comanches led by
     Loma (Victoria Horne), a half-breed.

370 Stagecoach to Denver (Republic 1946) R.G. Springsteen
        Red Ryder and Little Beaver (Bobby Blake) break up
     a land grab plot.

371 Under Nevada Skies (Republic 1946) Frank McDonald
        Roy Rogers leads a band of Indians, one of whom is
     Flying Eagle (George L. Lewis), to a victory over the
     villains.

                              1947

372 Along the Oregon Trail (Republic 1947) R.G. Springsteen
        Villains steal rifles to arm the Indians for an uprising.

373 Black Gold (Monogram 1947) Phil Karlson
        Charley Eagle (Anthony Quinn) and his wife Sarah
     (Katherine DeMille) become millionaires when oil is dis-
     covered on their land. They buy a race horse, adopt
     an orphaned Chinese boy, and their lives become more

complicated and troubled. A <u>Variety</u> critic comments:
"The Agnes Christine Johnston script, from an original
story by Caryl Coleman, is commendable in that there is
not a single Indian-uttered 'ugh' in the dialog. Plot
depicts Charley Eagle, uneducated redskin who loves nature, his horse and his wife." (25 June)

374 <u>Bowery Buckeroos</u> (Monogram 1947) William Beaudine
     In this Bowery Boys spoof of westerns, a <u>Variety</u>
critic notes that "even an Indian comes up with incongru-
ous lingo e.g. his analysis of a peculiar situation 'This
don't look kosher to me!'" (15 Oct)

375 <u>Buffalo Bill Rides Again</u> (Screen Guild 1947) Bernard B.
     Ray
     Buffalo Bill (Richard Arlen) thwarts the efforts of
the oil hungry villains who are inciting the Indians, three
of whom are Chief Brave Eagle (Chief Many Treaties),
White Mountain (Charles Stevens) and Young Bird (Shooting Star), to attack white settlers.

376 <u>Dangerous Venture</u> (UA 1947) George Archainbaud
     Hopalong Cassidy rescues an isolated tribe of Indians
descended from the Aztecs, one of whom is Talu (Patricia
Tate), after villains and a scientist try to exploit them.

377 <u>Last of the Redmen</u> (Columbia 1947) George Sherman
     Based on Cooper's <u>Last of the Mohicans</u>, this film
emphasizes Hawkeye (Michael O'Shea) and Uncas (Rich
Vallin) as heroes and Magua (Buster Crabbe) as the villain.

378 <u>The Last Round-Up</u> (Columbia 1947) John English
     To stop a possible uprising, Gene Autry gets new
and fertile lands for the Indians (led by a chief played
by Trevor Bardette), whose valuable land and water had
been appropriated by the whites from the town.

379 <u>Marshall of Cripple Creek</u> (Republic 1947) R.G. Spring-
     steen
     Little Beaver (Bobby Blake) is the young companion
of the hero, Red Ryder.

380 <u>Oregon Trail Scouts</u> (Republic 1947) R.G. Springsteen
     The villains try to break up the treaty Red Ryder

made with Indians by kidnapping the chief's grandson,
Little Beaver (Bobby Blake), but he rescues the boy
and takes him on as his companion.

381 The Prairie (Screen Guild 1947) Frank Wisbar
        In this film based on Cooper's novel, Indians threaten
     the heroes and massacre a pioneer family. The main
     Indian characters are Matoreeh (Chief Yowlachie) the
     villain, Eagle Feather (Chief Thunder Cloud) and Running
     Deer (Jay Silverheels).

382 Rustlers of Devil's Canyon (Republic 1947) R.G. Spring-
     steen
        This film also deals with the adventures of Red Ryder
     and Little Beaver. A Variety critic notes that "young
     Bobby Blake as an Indian kid, will appeal to the juves."
     (9 July)

383 The Senator Was Indiscreet (Universal 1947) George S.
     Kaufman
        This satiric film has a comic induction scene of In-
     dians, played by Oliver Blake, Chief Thunder Cloud,
     Chief Yowlachie, and Iron Eyes Cody.

384 Spoilers of the North (Republic 1947) Richard Sale
        The villain charms a half-breed woman, Laura Reed
     (Evelyn Ankers) and another woman in order to recruit
     Indians for illegal fishing.

385 Unconquered (Paramount 1947) Cecil B. De Mille
        The villain marries Hannah (Katherine DeMille), the
     daughter of Chief Guyasuto (Boris Karloff), to be able
     to exploit the Indians, who eventually attack the fort.
     A Variety critic comments on the melodrama of the plot:
     "The redskins are ruthless scalpers and ... when Cooper
     and Miss Goddard stay a death-dance ritual and escape
     over the treacherous falls, the customers will have to
     call forth their best Dick Tracy attitude." (24 Sept)
     A NYT critic notes that "it is also deplorably evident
     that Unconquered, in this year of grace, is as viciously
     anti-redskin as The Birth of a Nation was anti-Negro
     long years back." (19 Oct 1)

1948

386 Blazing Across the Pecos (Columbia 1948) Ray Nazarro
    The Durango Kid deals with gunrunning to the Indians, one of whom is played by Chief Thunder Cloud, and an Indian attack on a wagon train.

387 The Dude Goes West (AA 1948) Kurt Neumann
    In this satire of westerns, the Piute Indians of Running Wolf (Chief Yowlachie) capture the hero and his beloved.

388 Fort Apache (RKO 1948) John Ford
    Cochise (Miguel Inclan) and his Apaches, who had gone to Mexico because of their anger at a crooked Indian agent, wipe out a troop of cavalry led by an inexperienced officer. A Variety critic praises "the massacre scene where in the deadly drumming of the Indian ponies makes more potent the action that transpires." (10 Mar)

389 Fury at Furnace Creek (20th Cent-Fox 1948) Bruce Humberstone
    Spurred on by a villain who wants control of a silver mine, the Indians, one of whom is Little Dog (Jay Silverheels), massacre a cavalry troop at Fort Furnace Creek.

390 Indian Agent (RKO 1948) Lesley Selander
    When a crooked agent diverts funds for the reservation, the heroes come to the rescue of the Indians, two of whom are Red Fox (Noah Beery, Jr.) and Wavoka (Iron Eyes Cody).

391 The Paleface (Paramount 1948) Norman McLeod
    In this spoof of westerns, the cowardly hero (Bob Hope) foils an attack by Indians, three of whom are Chief Yellow Feather (Chief Yowlachie), Chief Iron Eyes (Iron Eyes Cody) and Wapato (Henry Brandon).

392 Rachel and the Stranger (RKO 1948) Norman Foster
    Indians attack homesteaders. A Variety critic comments: "A socko Indian raid ... is solid action stuff. Flaming arrows and war whoops pinpoint pioneer danger." (4 Aug)

393   Red River (UA 1948) Howard Hawks
        In this film about the founding of the Chisholm Trail,
      Comanches attack wagon trains. Quo (Chief Yowlachie)
      is the friend of the cook on the cattle drive. A Variety
      critic notes that "the picture realistically depicts ...
      the marauding Indians that bore down on the pioneers."
      (14 July)

                              1949

394   Apache Chief (Lippert 1949) Frank MacDonald
        Young Eagle (Alan Curtis) leads Indians who believe
      they can live in peace with whites, and Black Wolf
      (Russell Hayden) leads a band who attack wagon trains
      and settlers. At the end of the film the good Indian,
      Young Eagle, kills Black Wolf in a hand-to-hand fight
      and ends up with the beautiful Indian maiden, Watona
      (Carol Thurston). Other Indian characters are Big Crow
      (Trevor Bardette), Mohaska (Francis McDonald), Pani
      (Ted Hecht), Lame Bull (Roy Gordon), Grey Cloud (Billy
      Wilkerson), Tewa (Rodd Redwing), White Fawn (Hazel
      Nilsen), and a counciller (Charles Soldani).

395   Arctic Manhunt (Universal 1949) Ewing Scott
        An Eskimo woman, Narana (Carol Thurston), loses
      the white man she loves when he dies in the wilderness.

396   Canadian Pacific (20th Cent-Fox 1949) Edwin Marin
        An evil fur trader incites the Indians to attack the
      railroad builders.

397   Colorado Territory (Warner 1949) Raoul Walsh
        Colorado Carson (Virginia Mayo), a half-breed com-
      panion of the outlaw hero, dies with him at the end of
      the film.

398   The Cowboy and the Indians (Columbia 1949) John Eng-
      lish
        A crooked agent reduces a tribe of Indians to starva-
      tion by selling their food for his own profit and con-
      fiscating their stock. Gene Autry, with the aid of a half-
      breed Indian doctor, Nan Palmer (Sheila Ryan), gets food
      for the Indians and brings the villains to justice. At the
      end, Nan and the young Chief Lakohna (Jay Silverheels)

fall in love. The other Indian characters are Lucky Broken Arm (Claudia Drake), Broken Arm (Charles Stevens), Blue Eagle (Frank Lackteen) and Chief Long Arrow (Chief Yowlachie).

399 The Dalton Gang (Lippert 1949) Ford Beebe
    The tribe of Chief Irahu (George Lewis) helps the hero track down the villains.

400 Daughter of the West (Film Classics 1949) Harold Daniels
    An educated Navajo, Navo (Phillip Reed), who is in love with half-breed Lolita Moreno (Martha Vickers), brings to justice an Indian agent who uses liquor to trick the Indians out of mineral rights on the reservation. Other Indian characters in this film based on the Robert Callahan novel are Okeema (Marion Carney), Wateeka (Luz Alba), Yuba (Tony Barr), Indian Chief (Pedro de Cordoba), Ponca (Tommy Cook), and Medicine Man (Willow Bird). A Variety critic notes "Indian dances in full regalia, the native music and Reed's (Navo) trial by fire" will make the film appealing to children. (30 Mar)

401 Gun Runner (Monogram 1949) Lambert Hillyer
    Outlaws smuggle guns to hostile Indians in a film where "the action highlights are some scenes of Indian raids." (Var 15 June)

402 Ghost of Zorro (Republic 1949) Fred Brannon
    In this serial, Indians, one of whom is Yellow Hawk (Alex Montoya), join in attacks planned by the villain.

403 Laramie (Columbia 1949) Ray Nazarro
    The hero saves the day after gunrunners try to start an Indian war by setting up the murder of Chief Eagle (Shooting Star). Another Indian character is Running Wolf (Jay Silverheels).

404 Ma and Pa Kettle (Universal 1949) Charles Lamont
    Crowbar (Chief Yowlachie) and Geoduck (Lester Allen) are funny Indian friends of Pa. These characters, portrayed by different actors, appear in most of the Ma and Pa Kettle movies.

405 Massacre River (Monogram 1949) John Rawlins
    Indians led by Chief Yellowstone (Iron Eyes Cody) fight several battles with soldiers from an army post.

406   Mrs. Mike (UA 1949)
        Along with the hardships of life in northwestern Can-
      ada, the heroine must also deal with Indians, one of whom
      is Antenou (Chief Yowlachie).

407   Ranger of Cherokee Strip (Republic 1949) Philip Ford
        The hero helps out Joe Bearclaw (Douglas Kennedy),
      a Cherokee who has been framed by white cattlemen in-
      tent on pushing the Cherokee out of their territory.
      Other Indian characters are Chief Hunter (Monte Blue)
      and Tokata (Neyle Morrow), a schoolteacher.

408   Roll, Thunder, Roll (Eagle Lion 1949) Lewis Collins
        Red Ryder and Little Beaver (Don Kay Reynolds) stop
      some bandits. A Variety critic notes that "Don Kay
      Reynolds, as a fast riding Indian youngster, is given
      some sharp lines which will garner laughs, and his role
      as Ryder's junior detective should give juves some vi-
      carious participation in the wild and wooly adventures."
      (11 May) Little Beaver and Red Ryder also appear in
      three other 1949 films, Cowboy and the Prizefighter,
      The Fighting Redhead, and Ride, Ryder, Ride.

409   She Wore a Yellow Ribbon (RKO 1949) John Ford
        The Indians, two of whom are the wise old Pony That
      Walks (Chief Big Tree) and hostile Red Shirt (Noble John-
      son), destroy a stage depot and get some guns before
      the aging cavalry hero (John Wayne) and his men over-
      come them in their camp and thus stop an all-out war.

410   Stallion Canyon (Astor 1949) Harry Fraser
        Little Bear (Billy Hammond) is a friendly Indian who
      is falsely charged with murder. A Variety critic com-
      ments: "Billy Hammond rides well as Little Bear, but
      overdoes the heap-big Injun Talk." (1 June)

411   Tale of the Navajos (MGM 1949) John Haeseler
        As a narrator gives references to Indian gods and
      fragments of Navajo poetry, two boys, an Indian and a
      white search for a place mentioned in Navajo myth on
      the top of a remote mountain. A Variety reviewer notes
      that "a chance to do a much needed documentary on
      modern Indian life was muffed in this production." (2
      Mar)

411a <u>Tulsa</u> (Eagle Lion 1949) Stuart Heisler
      Redbird (Pedro Armendariz), an Indian in love with
the half-breed oil wildcatter, Cherokee (Susan Hayward),
becomes mentally distraught and starts fires in her oil
fields.

FILMS OF THE 1950s AND 1960s

A comment on Geronimo (1962) by a Variety reviewer epitomizes some of the changes in the portrayal of Indians during this era. Dismayed because the warlike Apaches of this film speak English like modern Americans and allow themselves to be "bossed about" by a white woman, he remarks: "They don't make Injun pictures the way they used to.... [This film] continues the screen's preoccupation with the philosophical, psychological and romantic ramifications of Indian matters in the late 19th century at the expense of the straight-from-the-shoulder, uninhibited action ingredients that characterized the early indifferent-to-racial-stereotypes westerns." (25 April)

This reviewer's lament for the old days shows how ingrained the image of proud, bloodthirsty Indians had become in the fiction of the westerns. Although hostile Indians, especially Apaches, Comanches and Sioux, remain a staple in the plots of westerns of this era, some notable films like Broken Arrow (1950) and Cheyenne Autumn (1964) show an increased sympathy for the Indian and a willingness to portray Indian leaders like Cochise, Dull Knife and Little Wolf as heroic central characters. In each film the main white characters have a respect for Indian culture and an understanding of how whites are destroying it.

The first example of cultural awareness in Broken Arrow comes at the beginning when the narrator, Tom Jeffords (James Stewart), says "when the Apaches speak they will be speaking in our language." Then, after dealing with the wounded Apache boy and the Apache warriors, Jeffords again comments, "I learned something that day. Apache women cried over their sons and Apache men had a sense of fair play." As the plot continues Jeffords deepens his appreciation of Apache culture through his study of the language with Juan, his friendship with Cochise and his marriage to Son-seeahray. In Cheyenne Autumn John Ford uses the Cheyenne language (or something like it) for dialogue between the Indian characters and introduces white characters who respect the Indians. The narrator, Tom Archer (Richard Widmark), shows his appreciation of the Cheyenne when he says to the Quaker woman who is working with them, "All you've seen are reservation Indians. The Cheyenne are the greatest fighters in the world, fierce, smart and meaner than sin." Archer's friend, the Polish sergeant, also shows an awareness of the Indians' predicament when he sees the parallel between the way the Kossacks had killed his people just because they were Poles, and the way the U.S. Army was exterminating the Indians just because they were Indians.

In addition to the use of narrators respectful of Indian culture, the filmmakers also embue the characters of Cochise, Dull Knife and Little Wolf with the intelligence to speak with simple eloquence and humor and the ability to fight with tactical shrewdness. In Cheyenne Autumn the Indian characters have such lines as "We are asked to remember much; the white man remembers nothing" or "Even a dog can go where he likes, but not a Cheyenne." In Broken Arrow, Cochise uses a pithy analogy in his speech to the assembled Apaches to persuade them to adapt to the coming of the whites: "If a big wind comes, a tree must bend or be lifted out by its roots." He shows his cleverness in a comment after Tom Jeffords makes a feeble attempt at shooting an arrow: "Never mind, by the time he's a grown man, he'll know how." Not only do these characters have verbal ability, but also military skill. A good example is Cochise's attack on the wagon train of soldiers. Seen from a vantage point above the wagons, Cochise directs the carefully orchestrated attack by having lookouts shoot arrows to signal the various waves of the attack during which the Indians quickly take over the wagons. The angles of the perspectives in the sequence clearly establish the superior military tactics of Cochise. In Cheyenne Autumn Dull Knife and Little Wolf show their skill when they direct the setting of grass fires behind which they can shoot at the advancing cavalry or when they position their people in a canyon--a move that allows them to keep the greater numbers of cavalry at bay. Such intelligence in these Indian characters, coupled with patterns of depicting them with close-ups and low-angle shots make them appear to be superior to most of the white characters.

Ultimately, however, this characterization leads to the

stereotypes of good and bad Indians and the image of the
noble savage. In <u>Broken Arrow</u>, just as the good Tom Jeffords
and General Howard contrast with evil townspeople so the good
Cochise is set off against the hostile Geronimo and other rebel
Apaches. Ultimately, Cochise is good because he is willing to
learn the ways of peace from a white friend and wise because
he accepts the inevitability of white dominance in the West,
whereas Geronimo is bad because he refuses to give in to the
whites (Biskind 230-245). In <u>Cheyenne Autumn</u> the good
whites, Archer, the Quaker woman he loves, and the Secretary of the Interior, are set against the cowboy who kills an
unarmed starving Cheyenne just because he always wanted to
kill an Indian, the fanatical German commander of Fort Robinson and the unfeeling politicians. Dull Knife and Little Wolf
contrast with the hostile young Red Shirt; they are good and
wise Indians because they are willing to accept the peace treaty
and reservation offered by the Secretary of the Interior whereas the rebellious Red Shirt is bad and appropriately punished
by death at the end.

    In fact, Cochise, Dull Knife and Little Wolf are so good
and noble that they are not believable fictional characters, as
several differences between the films and the books they are
based on can help to illustrate. For example, <u>Broken Arrow</u>
uses only a small part of the story of Cochise in Elliot Arnold's
<u>Blood Brother</u>; it never touches on Cochise's continuing de-
pression over the brutal killing of a Mexican or his drinking
and disillusion in his later years, all "negative" but humaniz-
ing elements of the character in the novel. In the film Cochise is so good in any way that will make him pleasing to
white audiences that his behavior prompts a <u>NYT</u> critic to
write: "No, we cannot accept this picture as either an exciting or reasonable account of the attitudes and ways of American Indians. They merit justice, but not such patronage"
(24 July 1950, 15). An example of a significant change in
<u>Cheyenne Autumn</u> occurs near the end when Little Wolf rides
into the camp of Dull Knife and kills Red Shirt for taking
one of his wives and then, seen from a low angle, rides off
into the horizon. In Mari Sandoz's historical version, a drunk-
en Little Wolf, for no immediate good reason, kills a Cheyenne
who had earlier flirted with his wives and then spends the
rest of his life in shameful exile. In each case, the filmmakers fall back on the noble savage image to provoke sympathy for these Indian leaders.

Sympathy for the Indians as victims never really gives
way to empathy, especially in Cheyenne Autumn. John Ford
makes his purpose in that film clear: "There are two sides
to every story, but I wanted to show their [the Indian's]
point of view for a change. Let's face it, we've treated them
very badly--it's a blot on our shield; we've cheated and
robbed, killed, murdered, massacred and everything else, but
they kill one white man and, God, out come the troops" (Bogdanovich 104). Ford uses the noble Indians to instill guilt
of the kind seen by a NYT critic who describes the film as
"a stark and eye-opening symbolization of a shameful tendency
that has prevailed in our national life--the tendency to be unjust and heartless to weaker peoples who get in the way of
manifest destiny" (24 Dec. 8). The Indians are only symbols
of white exploitation, not fictional characters significant as in-
dividuals. Although Broken Arrow shows more empathy than
Cheyenne Autumn, it also uses Indians as symbols of white
guilt, especially at the end when villains kill Sonseeahray and
Tom Jeffords has to ride off alone. Although both these films
mark a growth of awareness in the portrayal of Indians, common to a number of films in this era, sympathy doesn't give
way to real empathy until the contemporary period.

1950

412 Ambush (MGM 1950) Sam Wood
     The heroes rescue a white woman from the Apaches,
two of whom are Diablito (Charles Stevens) and Tana
(Chief Thunder Cloud). A Variety critic comments: "In
the yip-yip-yippee tradition of the better gallopers, Ho-
diak, Cowling and old fogie John McIntire lose their
scalps, redskin baddies Charles Stevens and Chief
Thunder Cloud get bumped off, too, and the Taylor lads
get their gals." (21 Dec)

413 Annie Get Your Gun (MGM 1950) George Sidney
     In this musical, Sitting Bull (J. Carrol Naish) is a
paternalistic friend of Annie Oakley, the star of Buffalo
Bill's Wild West Show who sings "I'm an Indian Too" as
she is adopted by the tribe during the show. Other Indian characters like Little Horse (Chief Yowlachie) figure
in the Indian attacks staged during the show.

414   Broken Arrow (20th Cent-Fox 1950) Delmer Daves
      Based on Elliot Arnold's Blood Brother, this film deals
      with the friendship of the hero and the Apache leader,
      Cochise. A Variety critic notes that "a group of Indians
      in supporting speaking roles add to the film's effective-
      nèss." (14 June) These characters are Goklia (Jay Sil-
      verheels), Juan (Billy Wilkerson), Nochale (Chris Yellow
      Bird), Pionsenay (J.W. Cody), Nahilzay (John War Eagle),
      Skinyea (Charles Soldani), and Teese (Iron Eyes Cody).
      (See pages 82-85 for further discussion.)

415   Cariboo Trail (20th Cent-Fox 1950) Edwin Marin
      Hostile Indians led by Chief White Buffalo (Fred Lib-
      by) attack white settlers.

416   Cherokee Uprising (Monogram 1950) Lewis Collins
      An evil Indian agent convinces the Indians, two of
      whom are Longknife (Iron Eyes Cody) and Gray Eagle
      (Chief Yowlachie), to attack wagon trains by giving them
      whiskey as a reward.

417   Cody of the Pony Express (Columbia 1950) Spencer Ben-
      net
      In chapters from this serial entitled "Captured by In-
      dians" and "The Fatal Arrow," Indians led by Chief Gray
      Cloud use guns supplied to them by outlaws to threaten
      the hero.

418   Colt 45 (Warner 1950) Edwin Marin
      The hero and some friendly Indians led by Walking
      Bear (Chief Thunder Cloud) bring the villains to justice.

419   Comanche Territory (Universal 1950) George Sherman
      When villains try to thwart the efforts of a good In-
      dian agent and gain control of a silver mine in Indian
      territory, the hero and heroine come to the rescue. A
      Variety critic comments: "This is one of the few recent
      screen vehicles in which the Indians are never cast as
      the villains. Spotting of the lawless white settlers in
      such a role gives a not unfamiliar plot a fresh twist."
      (5 April)

420   Davy Crockett, Indian Scout (UA 1950) Lew Landers
      The hero (George Montgomery), aided by Red Hawk
      (Phillip Reed) his loyal Indian friend wrongly suspected

to be a spy, rescues Army troops from the hostile Indians, three of whom are the evil Chief Lone Eagle (Robert
Barrat), High Tree (Billy Wilkerson), and Sleeping Fox
(Chief Thunder Cloud). Red Hawk eventually falls in
love with Frances (Ellen Drew), a half-breed who repents
her earlier part as a spy for the hostile Indians. A
Variety critic notes that the "Yarn hews to the formula
ingredients of howling Indians, ambushed wagon trains,
disloyal half-breeds and a slight touch of romance."
(11 Jan)

421 Devil's Doorway (MGM 1950) Anthony Mann
        Broken Lance Poole (Robert Taylor), an educated
Shoshone and Civil War hero, returns to his homeland
and starts a ranch which is then claimed by a villain.
After trying to settle the claim legally with the aid of a
female lawyer he loves, Broken Lance and many of his
people--one of whom is Thundercloud (Chief John Big
Tree)--are killed as they valiantly try to defend their
rights. A NYT critic comments: "Perhaps it is too late
now to change the course of fiction which has established
the American Indian as a ruthless savage, but our movie
makers appear to be endeavoring to right some of the
wrongs they themselves have done the red man over the
years." (10 Nov 35)

422 I Killed Geronimo (Eagle Lion 1950) John Hoffman
        The hero stops the smuggling of guns to the Apaches
and kills Geronimo (Chief Thunder Cloud) while the
Apaches are attacking a wagon train. A critic from National Parent Teacher comments: "Ironically enough,
though all the Indians in the picture are 'bad,' the one
character who is enacted with dignity and understanding
is the wicked Geronimo himself.... Today's social con-
science is made uncomfortable when the theme of a sup-
posedly historic picture seems to restate the old notion
that the only good Indian is a dead one." (Nov 36)

423 Indian Territory (Columbia 1950) John English
        Gene Autry brings to justice villains who have been
selling guns to the Indians, one of whom is Soma (Charles
Stevens), and leading them on raids against the whites.

424 The Iroquois Trail (UA 1950) Phil Karlson
        Based on characters from Cooper's novels, this film

deals with the exploits of Hawkeye (George Montgomery)
and Sagamore (Monte Blue), his faithful Indian guide,
as they deal with attacks by hostile Indians.

425 North of the Great Divide (Republic 1950) William Witney
         Roy Rogers, an Indian agent who is a blood brother
     of the Oseka tribe, helps the Indians by exposing vil-
     lains tampering with their salmon fishing rights and
     causing starvation on the reservation.

426 Raiders of Tomahawk Creek (Columbia 1950) Fred Sears
         The Durango Kid is an Indian agent who deals with
     the tribe of Chief Flying Arrow (Paul Marion).

427 Rio Grande (Republic 1950) John Ford
         Apaches raid a cavalry outpost and later the soldiers
     go into Mexico to rescue a group of children from them.
     A New York Times critic notes that "John Ford's con-
     tinuing war with the Red Man and his romance with the
     U.S. Cavalry ... shows a few signs of wear and tear in
     Rio Grande." (20 Nov 21)

428 Roar of the Iron Horse (Columbia 1950) Spencer Bennet,
     T. Carr
         In this serial, Indians threaten the whites in chapters
     called "Indian Attack," "Captured by Redskins" and
     "Redskin's Revenge."

429 Rocky Mountain (Warner 1950) William Keighley
         The hero (Errol Flynn) and his men rescue a woman
     from an Indian attack on a stagecoach by luring the In-
     dians away, but are killed themselves. A Variety critic
     comments: "The Indian raid on the stagecoach is excit-
     ing and the final clash when Flynn and his men go under
     redskin arrows is capital motion picture action." (4 Oct)

430 Ticket to Tomahawk (20th Cent-Fox 1950) Richard Sale
         Indians, some of whom are Pawnee (Chief Yowlachie),
     Trancos (Charles Stevens), Lone Eagle (John War Eagle),
     Crooked Knife (Chief Thunder Cloud) and Crazy Dog
     (Shooting Star), attack a train being hauled over the
     mountains by mules.

431 Train to Tombstone (Lippert 1950) William Berke
         Indians attack a train. A Variety critic notes that the

attacks, with the "same Injun repeatedly falling off his
pony," are "just plain funny in their ridiculousness."
(6 Sept)

432 The Traveling Saleswoman (Columbia 1950) Charles F.
Riesner
    In this comedy, the heroine gets involved in an Indian
uprising led by Chief Running Deer (Chief Thunder
Cloud).

433 Two Flags West (20th Cent-Fox 1950) Robert Wise
    After the commander of a fort deliberately kills the
son of a Kiowa chief, the Indians attack and gain vengeance by killing him in a fight that Time calls "about
as rousing an Indian fight as Hollywood has ever produced." (23 Oct 100-1)

434 Wagonmaster (RKO 1950) John Ford
    Navajos (one of whom is played by Jim Thorpe) threat-
en a wagon train but are appeased when the white man
who attacked a Navajo woman is punished.

435 Winchester '73 (Universal 1950) Anthony Mann
    The stories of the gun's passing through various lives,
one being a hostile Indian chief's, Young Bull (Rock Hudson), who leads his warriors on a raid of a U.S. Cavalry camp.

436 Young Daniel Boone (Monogram 1950) Reginald LeBorg
    The hero rescues two white girls from the Indians, two
of whom are Little Hawk (William Roy) and Walking Eagle
(Nipo T. Strongheart).

                          1951

437 Across the Wide Missouri (MGM 1951) William Wellman
    A white trapper married to a Blackfoot woman, Kamiah
(Maria Marques), tries to live in Indian land controlled
by Bear Ghost (Jack Holt) and Ironshirt (Richardo Mon-
talban), a hostile young warrior. After Chief Looking
Glass (J. Carrol Naish) is killed, the Indians attack and
Kamiah and Ironshirt die during the fighting. The film
contains scenes in which the Indians speak in their own
language.

438   Apache Drums (Universal 1951) Hugo Fregonese
      Apaches, one of whom is Chacho (Chinto Gusman), at-
      tack a town called Spanish Boot. A NYT critic notes
      that the film is "exciting fare when its green and red
      painted Indians, yelping and keening, ride to attack or
      literally bite the dust with authentic thuds." (7 May 22)

439   The Battle at Apache Pass (Universal 1951) George Sher-
      man
      An evil government agent conspires with Geronimo
      (Jay Silverheels) to break up a peace treaty between the
      whites and Cochise (Jeff Chandler), but peace is re-
      stored when Cochise defeats Geronimo in hand-to-hand
      combat. Other Indian characters are Nona (Susan Cabot),
      the wife of Cochise, and Little Elk (Tommy Cook). A
      Variety critic comments, "'Apache Pass' rates a large
      'A' for its handling of Indian character and customs.
      The redmen emerge as human beings instead of in the
      caricaturistic rigging to which they are usually fated."
      (2 April 1952)

440   Cavalry Scout (Monogram 1951) Lesley Selander
      The scout stops the villains from smuggling guns to
      hostile Sioux and Cheyenne.

441   Distant Drums (Warner 1951) Raoul Walsh
      The hero rescues prisoners taken by the Seminoles.
      They survive attacks and during the final one the hero
      kills the Seminole chief in a hand-to-hand duel under
      water.

442   Fort Defiance (UA 1951) John Rawlins
      Indians led by Brave Bear (Iron Eyes Cody) attack
      a small group of men and a stagecoach.

443   Jim Thorpe, All American (Warner 1951) Michael Curtiz
      This film tells the sad story of Jim Thorpe (Burt
      Lancaster), the Sauk and Fox Indian from Oklahoma who
      became a star in track, field, baseball, and football, and
      won the pentathlon and decathalon in the 1912 Olympics.
      After the loss of his Olympic medals, the decline of his
      professional football career, the death of his son and the
      divorce from his white wife, the sullen and frustrated
      Thorpe ends up driving a dump truck. A Variety critic
      notes that Burt Lancaster plays Thorpe "in the spirit of

the grim visaged, moody Indian." (20 June) Other In-
dian characters are Thorpe's friends, Little Boy (Jack
Big Head), Ed Guyac (Dick Wesson), his father Hiram
(Nestor Paiva), Wally Denny (Suni Warcloud) and Louis
Tewanema (Al Mejia).

444 The Last Outpost (Paramount 1951) Lewis R. Foster
    Even though Union soldiers had earlier fought against
the South with the help of Apaches and Geronimo (John
War Eagle), a brave Confederate cavalry troop saves a
Union post from an attack by the Indians of Chief Grey
Cloud (Charles Evans).

445 Little Big Horn (Lippert 1951) Charles Marquis Warren
    As a small cavalry squad tries to get to Custer to
warn him of the impending Sioux ambush, the Indians
kill all of them before they can complete their mission.

446 Navajo (Lippert 1951) Norman Foster
    A young Navajo boy, Little Son of the Hunter (Francis
Kee Teller), forced to go to a white school, escapes to a
canyon, tricks his pursuers, and then rescues them. A
Variety critic notes that the Indian actors from the reservation in Arizona give "the film the impact of complete
naturalness," (30 Jan 1952) and a critic from Parent and
Teacher comments: "Serious and moving, this drama
points to a new kind of Indian story vastly removed from
the commonplace melodrama of pioneer warfare." (Jan
1952, 37)

447 New Mexico (UA 1951) Irving Reis
    The hero tries to stop his friend, Chief Acuma (Ted
De Corsia), from fighting after villains break a treaty
but the Indians, armed with weapons supplied by a
crooked politician, finally make war.

448 Oh! Susanna (Republic 1951) Joseph Kane
    Indians led by Chief Pactola attack a fort, kill the
villain and his men but spare the man who has been trying to guard their treaty rights.

449 Only the Valiant (Warner 1951) Gordon Douglas
    After Apaches led by Tuscos (Michael Ansara) stage
a series of attacks on soldiers trying to hold a strategic
pass, the soldiers finally use a Gattling gun to defeat
them.

450 The Red Mountain (Paramount 1951) William Dieterle
     Influenced by General Quantrell, Utes make war on
     the whites. At the end the hero and a woman he has
     saved "are rescued in an all-out, shoot 'em-up, waving
     flags-charging cavalry, red-skins-bite-the-dust finale
     that uses every cliché in the book." (Var 14 Nov)

451 Santa Fe (Columbia 1951) Irving Pichel
     In one part Chief Longfeather (Chief Thunder Cloud)
     takes over an engine and gives those on the train a wild
     ride.

452 Slaughter Trail (RKO 1951) Irving Allen
     When a cavalry captain refuses to turn over to the
     Navajo chief bandits who have killed two of his people,
     the Indians attack the fort but kill only the bandits.

453 Snake River Desperadoes (Columbia 1951) Fred Sears
     The Durango Kid fights against villains disguised as
     Indians who are trying to start a war between the Indians
     and whites.

454 Tomahawk (Universal 1951) George Sherman
     After a cruel soldier kills the parents of Movahsectah
     (Susan Cabot) an Indian girl, the Sioux led by Red
     Cloud (John War Eagle) attack the soldiers of Fort Phil
     Kearney. A Commonweal critic comments on this film
     which deals with the Fetterman and Wagon Box massacres:
     "This is another in the current cycle of westerns that
     dares to speak up for the Indians and suggests that
     white men haven't always been too honorable in their
     dealings." (2 Mar 520)

455 Warpath (Paramount 1951) Byron Haskin
     The heroes flee from the Sioux to warn Custer. A
     Variety critic notes that "putting the cavalry against the
     Indians has become a rather common storybook." (6
     June)

456 When the Redskins Rode (Columbia 1951) Lew Landers
     Indians battle with colonials in a film that has "a gen-
     erous helping of skirmishes in which war-painted braves
     take on militiamen. Flintlocks flash and arrows twang in
     the best Hollywood tradition." (Var 9 May)

1952

457   Apache Country (Columbia 1952) George Archainbaud
      Gene Autry comes to the rescue when villains provide
guns and whiskey to the Indians and incite them to attack innocent whites.

458   Apache War Smoke (MGM 1952) Harold Kress
      Apaches attack a group of whites because one, a sup-
posed friend of the Indians, had robbed and killed several Apaches.

459   The Battles of Chief Pontiac (Realart 1952) Felix Feist
      When the evil leader of some Hessians tries to wipe
out the Ottawa of Chief Pontiac (Lon Chaney) by sending
them blankets infested with smallpox, the Indians get
their revenge by capturing him and wrapping him up in
the blankets. During this action the hero rescues a
white woman who is about to be raped by Hawkbill (Larry Chance).

460   Bend of the River (Universal 1952) Anthony Mann
      The hero, leading wagon train to Oregon, rescues it
by killing a group of hostile Indians in a night raid on
their camp.

461   The Big Sky (RKO 1952) Howard Hawks
      On a river journey the hero falls in love with Teal
Eye (Elizabeth Threatt), a Blackfoot woman whom the
leader has taken along so he will be able to trade with
her people. Accompanied by Poordevil (Hank Worden),
a somewhat crazy Blackfoot, the group is attacked by
Indians and the French. Other Indian characters are
Moleface (Frank de Kova) and Longface (Guy Wilkerson).

462   Brave Warrior (Columbia 1952) Spencer G. Bennet
      The hero, aided by the peace-loving Tecumseh (Jay
Silverheels), deals with villains who are turning the Indians, two of whom are the Prophet (Michael Ansara)
and Chief Little Cloud (Billy Wilkerson), against the
whites. A Variety critic notes that "Silverheels makes
a vivid characterization of Tecumseh, the Shawnee chief."
(14 May)

463   Buffalo Bill in Tomahawk Territory (UA 1952) Bernard B.
      Ray

Villains after gold on Indian land try to get the Army
to drive the Sioux away by disguising themselves as Indians and attacking wagon trains. Buffalo Bill (Clayton
Moore) discovers the plot and thus keeps the peace with
Chief White Cloud (Rodd Redwing) of the Sioux.

464   Bugles in the Afternoon (Warner 1952) Roy Rowland
Sioux Indians attack Fort Lincoln and defeat Custer
(Sheb Wooley) at the Battle of Little Big Horn. A NYT
critic feels that "this film should be given back to the
Indians. And judging by the expressions of the con-
tributing Sioux, they want no part of it." (5 Mar 32)

465   Desert Pursuit (Monogram 1952) George Blair
At first Mission Indians think the villains, who are
riding camels in pursuit of an innocent couple, are the
Three Wise Men, but then the next day they see the
truth and rescue the couple.

466   Flaming Feather (Paramount 1952) Ray Enright
Indians raid, fight with the cavalry, ambush, and attack the villain in his cliff dwelling hideout, where Tur-
quoise (Carol Thurston), an Indian woman he had rejected, kills him.

467   Fort Osage (Monogram 1952) Lesley Selander
After villains break a treaty, the Osage Indians attack a wagon train, but they punish only the villains and
let the rest of the wagons go on.

468   The Half Breed (RKO 1952) Stuart Gilmore
Charlie Wolf (Jack Buetel), an Apache half-breed,
joins the hero in bringing to justice villains who are trying to start trouble so they can get gold on the reservation. A Variety critic notes the half-breed's "vocabulary
is primarily limited to exclamations of 'Ugh' and sentences
of no more than three or four words at most," (16 April)
and a NYT reviewer comments: "While 'The Half Breed'
is immensely dull, it does profess concern for the Indians of 1867, which is commendable but hardly timely.
Perhaps it will give someone an idea for a motion picture
about the plight of the contemporary Indian, the Navajos
of the Southwest, for instance." (5 July 7)

469   Hiawatha (Monogram 1952) Kurt Neumann

Based on Longfellow's poem, this film deals with the
love of the Ojibwa Indian, Hiawatha (Vince Edwards),
and the Sioux woman, Minnehaha (Yvette Dugay), and the
conflicts between the tribes caused by Puk Keewis (Keith
Larsen), an Ojibway brave who wants war. Hiawatha
stops the war and finally his tribe allows Minnehaha to
be his bride.

470 Indian Uprising (Columbia 1952) Ray Nazarro
The hero prevents an Apache uprising incited by villains after gold on Indian land. At the end Geronimo is
tricked into surrendering. A Variety critic comments:
"This basic good vs evil motivation has been done before.
As usual the hero is the peacekeeper, the villains are the
exploiters and the Indians are the losers." (26 Dec 1951)

471 Laramie Mountains (Columbia 1952) Ray Nazarro
When villains try to start a war to get the gold of
the Indians, two of whom are Swift Eagle (Jock Mahoney)
and Chief Lone Tree (John War Eagle), the Durango Kid
comes to the rescue.

472 Pony Soldier (20th Cent-Fox 1952) Joseph Newman
A Mountie and his half-breed guide, Natayo (Thomas
Gomez), try to stop the Northern Cree from fighting in
Montana. Befriended by Chief Standing Bear (Stuart
Randall) and an Indian boy Comes Running (Anthony
Numkena), and opposed by Konah (Cameron Mitchell), a
hostile sub-chief who is finally killed by Comes Running,
the hero eventually leads them back to Canada. Other
Indian characters are White Moon (Adeline De Walt Reynolds), Roks-Ki (Muriel Landers), Shemawgun (Grady
Galloway), Medicine Man (Nipo T. Strongheart), and
Katatatsi (Carlos Loya). Anthony Numkena Sr., John
War Eagle, Chief Bright Fire and Chief Thundersky also
play Indians. A NYT critic comments: "Anything but
the old-time movie redskins, full of festering resentments
and booze, these are fine and upstanding representatives
of a racial minority. They are all the time holding solemn
councils at which everyone has a chance to talk (in stilted,
but richly flowery English) and they are great ones for
keeping their words." (20 Dec 15)

473 Red Snow (Columbia 1952) Boris Petroff, Harry Franklin
An Eskimo soldier, Sgt. Koovuk (Ray Mala), finds that

the Russians are developing a new weapon. Other Eskimo characters are his wife Alak (Gloria Saunders), Chief
Nanu (Robert Bice) and Tuglu (Philip Ahn). A Variety
critic notes that the film contains "stock footage showing
Eskimos hunting, playing, fleeing an ice break up and
fighting off a polar bear, etc." (2 July)

474   The Savage (Paramount 1952) George Marshall
        Warbonnet (Charlton Heston), a white man brought
up by the Sioux, finally sides with the whites in order
to show his Indian friends that peace is the best course.
In doing this, he goes to his white lover and leaves behind Luta (Joan Taylor), who loves him. Other Indian
characters are Running Dog (Donald Porter), Iron
Breast (Ted De Corsia), Yellow Eagle (Ian Mac Donald),
Pehangi (Angela Clarke), and Long Mine (Larry Tolan).

475   Son of Geronimo (Columbia 1952) Spencer Bennet
        In serial chapters like "Indian Ambush," "On the War-
path," and "Trapped in a Flaming Tepee," Apaches,
two of whom are Porico (Rodd Redwing) and Geronimo
(Chief Yowlachie), attack wagon trains but then turn
against their outlaw allies.

476   Son of Paleface (Paramount 1952) Frank Tashlin
        Indians on the warpath led by their chief (Iron Eyes
Cody), are one of the threats to the hero (Bob Hope)
in this burlesque of westerns.

477   The Story of Will Rogers (Warner 1952) Michael Curtiz
        This film is a sympathetic biography of the famous
part-Indian humorist.

478   Wagons West (Monogram 1952) Ford Beebe
        Cheyenne, armed with smuggled rifles and led by
Chief Black Kettle (John Parrish) and Kaw Chief (Charles
Stevens), attack a wagon train heading for California.

479   Westward the Women (MGM 1952) William Wellman
        The heroines show their strength by dealing with In-
dian attacks.

480   The Wild North (MGM 1952) Andrew Marton
        An Indian girl (Cyd Charisse), from a tribe whose
chief is played by John War Eagle, is in love with the

hero. A Newsweek critic notes that "Cyd Charisse, as a docile Indian maiden, supplies a touch of academic sex appeal." (17 Mar 96)

1953

481 Ambush at Tomahawk Gap (Columbia 1953) Fred Sears
     Apaches shooting flaming arrows attack the whites.

482 Arrowhead (Paramount 1953) Charles Marquis Warren
     The hero, raised by the Apaches and loved by Nita (Katy Jurado), becomes an Indian hater, but eventually brings peace when he defeats the warlike young leader of the Apache, Toriano (Jack Palance). A NYT critic comments: "Whatever feelings of friendship for the American Indian may have been shown in a few open-minded Hollywood Westerns lately, it is plain that Producer Nat Holt is having no truck with any such ideas. To him an Indian is still a treacherous dog." (16 Sept 38)

483 Captain John Smith and Pocahontas (UA 1953) Lew Landers
     After Pocahontas (Jody Lawrence) overcomes the plotting of the hostile Opechanco (Stuart Randall), she gets permission from her father, Powatan (Douglass Dumbrille), to marry John Smith. Other Indian characters are Nantaques (Shepard Menken), Mawhis (Franchesca di Scaffa) and Lacuma (Joan Nixon).

484 The Charge at Feather River (Warner 1953) Gordon Douglas
     After the hero rescues two women, one of whom has fallen in love with Chief Thunder Hawk (Fred Carson), the Indians give chase and attack at the river. This 3D film thrills the audience with flying arrows, spears and tomahawks.

485 Column South (Universal 1953) Frederick de Cordova
     When the villain tries to get Menquito (Dennis Weaver) and his Navajo tribesmen to fight in order to cover up his defection to the Confederacy, the hero foils his plans. A Variety critic notes that "it's another of those Cavalry and Indians, North vs South entries laid in the west in

the period before the start of the War between the States."
(13 May)

486 The Command (Warner 1953) David Butler
     Indians fight the cavalry and attack in a sequence
which prompts a Newsweek critic to note that "rampaging
Indians have never ringed a wagon train in such pano-
ramic fury." (1 Feb 76)

487 Conquest of Cochise (Columbia 1953) William Castle
     Cochise (John Hodiak) joins with the Comanches in
raids on the Mexicans but then opts for peace and helps
the hero defeat his former allies. Other Indian characters in "this sympathetic treatment of the problems of
Indians," (Var. 26 Aug) are Terua (Carol Thurston),
Red Knife (Rodd Redwing), and Running Cougar (Joseph
Waring).

488 Escape from Fort Bravo (MGM 1953) John Sturges
     Mescalero Apaches attack a small group of soldiers and
a woman pinned down in a shallow desert wash. A Variety critic comments: "It diverges from the usual Indian
battle seen on film by having the redskins use regular
artillery tactics in pinpointing their target for barrages
of arrows." (11 Nov)

489 Fort Ti (Columbia 1953) William Castle
     Indians attack the fort. A married Indian woman,
Running Otter (Phyllis Fowler), loves the hero, but at
the end he chooses a white woman.

490 Fort Vengeance (Allied Artists 1953) Lesley Selander
     Sitting Bull (Michael Granger) and his Sioux are in
Canada trying to stir up the peaceful Blackfoot led by
Crowfoot (Morris Ankrum), whose son Eagle Heart (Paul
Marion) has been unjustly accused of murder. The hero,
a Mountie, finds the real murderer (his own brother)
and thereby averts the uprising.

491 The Great Sioux Uprising (Universal 1953) Lloyd Bacon
     The hero comes to the rescue when villains steal
horses from Red Cloud (John War Eagle) and his Sioux
in order to start a fight. The plot is further complicated by a Confederate Indian soldier who wants the Indians to attack the Union troops. A reviewer from Nat-

ural History comments that the Indians "supply background
for the machinations of the villain, and well-intentioned
but mistaken menace for the principal characters. These
are Hollywood Indians and are always seen dressed in
their best, but at least they are represented as humans
with normal reactions." (June 286)

492 Hondo (Warner 1953) John Farrow
     The hero (John Wayne) who is part Indian, fights
Apaches led by Vittorio (Michael Pate) and Silva (Rudolfo Acosta) in a film where there is enough "short
range shooting of Indians to satisfy even a generation
of children who have been nourished on the blood of
afternoon TV programs." (Time 14 Dec 112) A Variety
critic notes that "Vittorio ... is shown as a just leader
concerned about the problems of his people and be-
wildered by the white man's violation of treaties." (25
Nov)

493 Jack McCall, Desperado (Columbia 1953) Sidney Salkow
     Villains steal land with gold on it from the Sioux, two
of whom are Grey Eagle (Eugene Iglesias) and Red Cloud
(Jay Silverheels). A Variety critic notes that "chase
scenes and the ambush sequences, where Indians, portrayed along favorable lines, are massacred, are handled
effectively." (25 Mar)

494 Last of the Comanches (Columbia 1953) Andre De Toth
     When Comanches led by Black Cloud (John War Eagle)
attack a small group of whites trapped in an abandoned
mission, Little Knife (Johnny Stewart), an Indian treated
well by whites in the past, helps to rescue them.

495 The Nebraskan (Columbia 1953) Fred Sears
     An army scout protects his Indian aide, Wingfoot
(Maurice Jara) who is accused of killing an Indian chief,
from evil whites and the Indians led by Spotted Bear
(Jay Silverheels) and Yellow Knife (Pat Hogan).

496 Old Overland Trail (Republic 1953) William Witney
     A villain uses whiskey and rifles to stir up Apaches
led by Black Hawk (Leonard Nimoy). An Indian agent
comes to the rescue and the Indians gain revenge by
killing the villain.

497   The Pathfinder (Columbia 1953) Sidney Salkow
         In this film based on Cooper's novel, the hero (George
      Montgomery), aided by Chingachgook (Jay Silverheels)
      and Uncas (Ed Coch, Jr.) spy on the French for the
      British. Chief Arrowhead (Rodd Redwing) is the leader
      of the hostile Mingos and Lokawa (Elena Verdugo) is the
      Indian wife of a British soldier. Other Indian charac-
      ters are Eagle Feather (Chief Yowlachie), Togamak (Ross
      Conklin), Ka-letan (Vi Ingraham).

498   Peter Pan (RKO 1953) Hamilton Luske, Clyde Geronimi,
      Wilfred Jackson
         In this Disney animated version, Candy Candido is
      the bass voice of the Indian Chief who protects Peter
      Pan and the children. Also included is the song, "What
      Makes the Red Man Red," which is sung during a powwow
      at the Indian village.

499   Pony Express (Paramount 1953) Jerry Hopper
         The hero, Buffalo Bill Cody (Charlton Heston), has
      a hand-to-hand battle with Chief Yellow Hand (Pat Hogan)
      after the Indians captured him.

500   Saginaw Trail (Columbia 1953) George Archainbaud
         A villain disguises himself as an Indian and hires
      renegade Indians to attack settlers in the Michigan woods.
      Indian characters are Red Bird (John War Eagle), the
      Huron (Rodd Redwing) and the Fox (Billy Wilkerson).

501   Seminole (Universal 1953) Budd Boetticher
         After the peaceful Osceola (Anthony Quinn) is killed
      when he is tricked into the fort, the hero faces a trial
      for the murder of his boyhood friend until Katjeck (Hugh
      O'Brian), a Seminole chief, admits to the killing. An
      Indian reviewer for Natural History comments: "Applause
      for Howard Christie, the producer of an unpretentious
      but new type of Indian picture, for he has broken away
      from a worn-out pattern. For the last 20 years 'savages'
      have whooped, danced, and chased their enemies while
      their noble chief looked on as stoic as a cigar-store In-
      dian." (April 190)

502   The Stand at Apache River (Universal 1953) Lee Sholem
         A small band of Apaches led by Cara Blanca (Edgar
      Barrier) and Deadhorse (Forrest Lewis) attack some people
      at a stagecoach station.

503 The Tall Texan (Lippert 1953) Elmo Williams
     Indians, one of whom is Jaqui (George Steele), at-
tacks whites who are after the gold on Indian land.

504 Tumbleweed (Universal 1953) Nathan Juran
     Yaqui Indians, two of whom are Aguila (Ralph Moody)
and Tigre (Eugene Iglesias), attack the whites, but one
of the Indians, whom the hero had helped before, comes
to his rescue.

505 War Paint (UA 1953) Lesley Selander
     The hero struggles to get a treaty to the Indians,
two of whom are Taslik (Keith Larsen) and Wanima (Joan
Taylor), in time to avert a war.

1954

506 Apache (UA 1954) Robert Aldrich
     Massai (Burt Lancaster), one of Geronimo's (Monte
Blue) men, escapes while being taken to prison and
wages war against the army. Later, when Massai stops
fighting, the government doesn't punish him because his
actions were part of a declared war, not just revenge.
At the end he and the Indian woman he loves, Nalinle
(Jean Peters), decide to work together for his tribe in
peace. A Variety critic comments on this film based on
the Paul I. Wellman novel: "Lancaster and Miss Peters
play their Indian roles understandingly without usual
screen stereotyping. As played, these two top characters are humans, surprisingly loquacious in contrast to
usual clipped redskin portrayals." (30 June)

507 Arrow in the Dust (Allied Artists 1954) Lesley Selander
     The hero stops Pawnee Indian attacks on a wagon
train by destroying the guns and ammunition they are
after. A NYT critic describes the point of the film as
"the threat of murderous red savages intent on wiping
out settlers and troopers." (1 May 13)

508 Battle of Rouge River (Columbia 1954) William Castle
     After the villain gets the Indians of Chief Mike
(Michael Granger) in a warlike mood so he can exploit
their resources, the hero intervenes and makes peace
with them.

509 The Black Dakotas (Columbia 1954) Ray Nazarro
      A Southerner disguised as a Yankee incites the Sioux,
      three of whom are War Cloud (John War Eagle), Black
      Buffalo (Jay Silverheels) and Spotted Deer (George Key-
      mas), to fight the Union soldiers. A NYT critic com-
      ments: "A recent, widespread "gimmick" for Westerns,
      low-budget and high, has been the Civil War, with sym-
      pathizers lining up for both sides and the poor Indian
      used as a buffer." (2 Oct 21)

510 Broken Lance (20th Cent-Fox 1954) Edward Dmytryk
      A white man married to an Indian woman, Senora
      Devereaux (Katy Jurado), struggles against the contempt
      and hatred for his wife and half-breed son Joe (Robert
      Wagner) who is in love with a white woman. A Variety
      critic notes that the Indian wife's "role is endowed with
      a womanly understanding that is one of the film's better
      points." (28 July)

511 Cattle Queen of Montana (RKO 1954) Allan Dwan
      Aided by Colorados, the college-educated chief of the
      Blackfoot, the hero helps the heroine fight the villain
      and whiskey-drinking Blackfoot led by the hostile Natcha-
      koa (Anthony Caruso). Other Indian characters are
      Starfire (Yvette Dugay) and Powhani (Rodd Redwing).
      A Variety critic comments: "In the picture's favor (but
      this seems to be a trend lately in Indian territory stories)
      is an attempt to depict the problems of the Redmen in
      fighting the encroachment of their land by the white set-
      tlers. The Indians are not all evil, scalp-hunting devils."
      (17 Nov)

512 Drum Beat (Warner 1954) Delmer Daves
      When the hero tries for a treaty with Modoc Indians,
      led by the rebellious Captain Jack (Charles Bronson),
      Manok (Anthony Caruso) a friendly Modoc, helps him,
      as does Toby (Marisa Pavan) a young Indian woman who
      gives her life to save him.

513 Drums Across the River (Universal 1954) Nathan Juran
      The villain starts trouble with Utes, three of whom
      are Taos (Jay Silverheels), Chief Owray (Morris Ankrum)
      and Red Knife (Ken Terrell), to get at Indian gold. The
      hero, who hates Indians because his mother had been
      killed by one, eventually changes his mind and works with
      the friendly chief to bring peace.

514 Four Guns to the Border (Universal 1954) Richard Carlson
     Yaqui (Jay Silverheels) is one of the four central characters.

515 Garden of Evil (20th Cent-Fox 1954) Henry Hathaway
     Apaches ambush a group of outlaws.

516 Man with the Steel Whip (Republic 1954) Franklin Adreon
     In chapters like "Redskin Raiders," a villain who is after the Indian's gold persuades them to make trouble, until the hero wins them over and stops him.

517 Massacre Canyon (Columbia 1954) Fred Sears
     Apaches, led by Black Eagle (Steve Ritch) and Running Horse (Chris Alcaide), attack a wagon train carrying rifles.

518 Overland Pacific (UA 1954) Fred Sears
     The villain gives rifles to the Indians led by Chief Dark Thunder (Pat Hogan) and keeps them on the warpath to force the railroaders to build on his land.

519 River of No Return (20th Cent-Fox 1954) Otto Preminger
     Indians use rocks and arrows to attack a raft in a film where "the plot is best summed up by a recurrent phrase in the picture: 'The country's alive with Indians,' ... There is a 'red-man-infested landscape' in the movie." (Time 17 May 89)

520 Rose Marie (MGM 1954) Mervyn LeRoy
     Wanda (Joan Taylor), an Indian woman, appears in "Totem Tom Tom," an Indian dance described by a NYT critic: "A vast swarm of Culver City red-men stomp about and point spears in the air while Joan Taylor as a jilted Indian maiden squirms and thrashes to the wild beat of the drums." (2 Apr 22)

521 Saskatchewan (Universal 1954) Raoul Walsh
     The hero, a Mountie who had been raised by Indians, tries to stop the Sioux of Sitting Bull from inciting the friendly Canadian Cree into a war. The Indian characters are Cajou (Jay Silverheels), Chief Dark Cloud (Antonio Moreno), and Spotted Eagle (Anthony Caruso). A NYT critic comments: "Some of the standard Indian fight-

ing is grandly pictorial, too, with audacious extras making wild leaps and dying in lovely agonies." (11 Mar
26)

522   The Siege at Red River (20th Cent-Fox 1954) Rudolph
      Mate
          The villain sells a Gattling gun to hostile Indians led
      by Chief Yellow Hawk (Rico Alaniz) and helps them at-
      tack a Union fort.

523   Sitting Bull (UA 1954) Sidney Salkow
          The hero tries to make peace with the Sioux, led by
      Sitting Bull (J. Carrol Naish) who also wants peace.
      However, he gets in trouble when the Indian-hating
      Custer (Douglas Kennedy) and an Indian agent start a
      war. At the end, Sitting Bull exonerates him and then
      makes a peace treaty with President Grant. Other Indian
      characters are Crazy Horse (Iron Eyes Cody) and Young
      Buffalo (Felix Gonzalez).

524   Southwest Passage (UA 1954) Ray Nazarro
          Indians, who first think camels are a kind of god,
      later attack the whites traveling on them.

525   Taza, Son of Cochise (Universal 1954) Douglas Sirk
          In this sequel to Broken Arrow, Taza (Rock Hudson)
      tries to keep the peace, but his brother Naiche (Bart
      Roberts) convinces the tribe to join with the hostile
      Geronimo (Ian MacDonald) and Grey Eagle (Morris Ankrum).
      When they attack the cavalry, Taza and his soldier friend
      Captain Barnett come to the rescue and restore the peace.
      Other Indian characters are Oona (Barbara Rush) the
      daughter of Grey Eagle, Chato (Eugene Igelesias), Skinja
      (James Van Horn) and Kocha (Charles Horvath). A
      Newsweek critic comments: "Taza, Son of Cochise is an-
      other chapter in Hollywood's long and truculent argument
      with the American Indian. This one, like many others,
      pays a kind of service to the idea that Indians may be
      men of merit, but as usual they take a numerical licking."
      (1 Mar 80)

526   They Rode West (Columbia 1954) Phil Karlson
          Kiowa who join the hostile Comanches of Chief Quanah
      Parker (John War Eagle) threaten the hero, but he keeps
      the peace when he successfully operates on the Kiowa

chief's son who is married to a white woman raised by
his tribe. Other Indian characters are Satanta (Stuart
Randall), Red Wolf (Eugene Igelsias), Asatai (Frank de
Kova) and Spotted Wolf (Maurice Jara).

527   War Arrow (Universal 1954) George Sherman
        The hero, with the help of Seminoles led by Magro
      (Henry Brandon), puts down a Kiowa uprising incited
      by a villain and led by Santanta (Jay Silverheels). Avis
      (Susan Ball), the daughter of Magro, is described by a
      Variety critic as "a fiery Seminole princess." (9 Dec
      1953)

528   The Yellow Tomahawk (UA 1954) Lesley Selander
        After an evil officer kills Indian women and children
      for no reason and breaks a treaty by planning to build
      a fort in Indian country, Fire Knife (Lee Van Cleef) de-
      clares war. After many whites are killed, the hero, a
      friend of Fire Knife, saves the survivors but kills his
      friend in the process. Other Indian characters are Tonio
      (Noah Beery, Jr.) and his woman, Honey Bear (Rita
      Moreno). A Variety critic notes that "The Harold Jack
      Bloom story takes the redskins' side to show provocation
      for their attacks on a cavalry encampment and this angle
      is played up properly in the script." (19 May)

                              1955

529   Apache Ambush (Columbia 1955) Fred Sears
        Apaches join with Mexican bandits in raids on the
      whites. A Variety critic comments: "One thing about
      this pic; it won't make the distributor very popular in
      Mexico or with Indians. Both are shown up in the worst
      possible light." (10 Aug)

530   Apache Woman (American 1955) Roger Corman
        The hero finds out that murders thought to be com-
      mitted by reservation Apaches were actually done by
      Armand (Lance Fuller), a crazed, college educated half-
      breed and his sister (Joan Taylor). A Variety critic
      notes that "Miss Taylor, who can now play an Indian
      without a feather, is particularly outstanding in a fiery
      portrayal" of the half-breed femme fatale. (10 Dec)

531 Battle Cry (Warner 1955) Raoul Walsh
     Crazy Horse (Felix Noriego), an Indian soldier, is a
common character type in World War II films.

532 Chief Crazy Horse (Universal 1955) George Sherman
     Through the influence of a white friend and his wife,
Black Shawl (Susan Ball), Crazy Horse (Victor Mature),
who sees himself as the prophesized leader of the Lakota-
Sioux, finally makes peace only to be killed by an Indian
soldier, Little Big Man (Ray Danton). Other Indian characters are Flying Hawk (Keith Larsen), Worm (Paul Guil-
foyle), Spotted Tail (Robert Warwick), Red Cloud (Morris Ankrum), Old Man Afraid (Stuart Randall), Dull
Knife(Pat Hogan) and He Dog (Henry Wills). A NYT
critic comments: "Mr. Mature stalks grimly and grandly,
with his head up and nostrils flanged, looking less like
a flesh-and-blood Indian than like one of the cigar-store
tribe. A sense of his being a noble redman, which is
what this film was meant to convey, depends wholly upon
how susceptible one is to the wooden cliché." (28 April
25) However, a Time critic notes that the film "... pays
a Technicolor installment on Hollywood's mountain of debt
to the American Indian: after years of getting clobbered,
the redskins this time win three battles in a row over
the U.S. cavalry." (30 May 86)

533 Davy Crockett--King of the Wild Frontier (Buena Vista
     1955) Norman Foster
     The first part of this film deals with Crockett's (Fess
Parker) Indian fighting, in which he wins the respect
of Chief Red Stick (Pat Hogan). Another Indian character is Charles Two Shirts (Jeff Thompson).

534 The Far Horizons (Paramount 1955) Rudolph Mate
     Based on the novel Sacajawea of the Shoshones by
Della G. Emmons, this film deals with the Lewis and
Clark expedition and the romance between Clark (Charlton Heston) and Sacajawea (Donna Reed). After helping
the expedition reach its goal despite many Indian attacks,
such as that of Chief Camillo, Sacajawea finally decides
to leave Clark. One critic finds Donna Reed to be "a
high fashion pulse-thumper turned out in beautifully
tailored buckskins." (Time 6 June 110)

535 Fort Yuma (UA 1955) Lesley Selander

After soldiers kill his father at a peace parley, Mangas (Abel Fernandez), the young Apache chief, tries to
attack the fort by disguising his men as soldiers.   In
the fort an Indian-hating officer is in love with Francesca
(Joan Taylor), an Apache woman whose brother (John
Hudson) is a scout for the soldiers.

536 Foxfire (Universal 1955) Joseph Pevney
Jonathan Dartland (Jeff Chandler), a half-breed
Apache mining engineer whose mother is Saba (Celia Lov-
sky), has troubles with his white wife. A Saturday
Review critic notes that the script "probes unusually
deep in analyzing the position of women in an Apache
tribe and their relation to their men, with one beautifully handled sequence in which the withered Indian mother
explains by indirection the ways of her people to the be-
wildered young wife." (30 July 26)

537 The Gun That Won the West (Columbia 1955) William
Castle
The hero, using the Springfield rifle, subdues the
Sioux led by Chief Red Cloud (Robert Bice) and Afraid
of Horses (Michael Morgan) in "another story of how 'we'
won the West." (Var 20 July)

538 The Indian Fighter (UA 1955) Andre De Toth
When the hero falls in love with Onahti (Elsa Martinel-
li), the Chief's beautiful daughter, and neglects his duties
as a wagonmaster, a villain after gold uses whiskey to
start trouble with the Sioux of Red Cloud (Eduard Franz).
At the end the hero keeps the peace by delivering the
villain to the Indians. A Newsweek critic, referring to
a statement in the film that there can be no peace between
red and white men, comments, "This is just as well for
Hollywood, which relies on scalping and skulking for a
sizable portion of its annual output. Its tribesmen have,
of late, been getting nobler and nobler, and occasionally
they even come out all right, always with the understanding white man passing the pipe of peace." (9 Jan 1956
71)

539 Kiss of Fire (Universal 1955) Joseph M. Newman
Acosta (Henry Rowland) and his tribe threaten whites
in the frontier of the Southwest.

540   The Last Frontier (Columbia 1955) Anthony Mann
      The hero, with his Indian companion, Mungo (Pat Ho-
gan), fight the Indians of Red Cloud (Manuel Donde)
and Spotted Elk (William Calles). An NYT critic, noting
that in the early films the cavalry was good and Indians
were bad until "civilization" reversed the images, remarks
that in this film "civilization has got so far that every-
body is ornery." (8 Dec 1)

541   The Man from Laramie (Columbia 1955) Anthony Mann
      A villain sells repeating rifles to the Apaches and
they use them to kill the hero's brother.

542   Many Rivers to Cross (MGM 1955) Roy Rowland
      The hero rescues his beloved from the Indians, two
of whom are Sandak (Ralph Moody) and Slangoh (Abel
Fernandez).

543   Masterson of Kansas (Columbia 1955) William Castle
      A villain tries to stop the Indians of Yellow Hawk (Jay
Silverheels) from getting rich grasslands by framing the
white man who is Yellow Hawk's friend.

544   Santa Fe Passage (Republic 1955) William Witney
      Chief Satank (George Keymas) and his Kiowa tribe
attack a group which includes the hero, who hates Indians because they killed his family; the woman he loves,
Aurlie (Faith Domergue), a half-breed; and her mother,
Ptewaquin (Irene Tedrow).

545   Seminole Uprising (Columbia 1955) Earl Bellamy
      After Seminoles led by Black Cat (Steve Ritch) es-
cape from a Florida reservation and go on raids in Texas,
the hero rescues a woman from them and kills Black Cat.

546   Seven Cities of Gold (20th Cent-Fox 1955) Robert Webb
      Father Junipero Serra brings religion to the Indians
but when the villain seduces Ula (Rita Moreno), a young
Indian woman, their leader Matuwir (Jeffrey Hunter),
threatens war until the man gives himself up. A NYT
critic comments: "We have seldom seen such acrobatic
Indians as the painted and feathered demons who pop up
here to harass and battle the Spaniards, until Father
Serra passes a few small 'miracles.' Fortunately, they
speak English almost as well as the Spaniards, so he is
able to communicate." (8 Oct 2)

547   Shotgun (Allied Artists 1955) Lesley Selander
      The hero rescues a woman captured by the Apaches
      of Delgadito (Paul Marion).

548   Smoke Signal (Universal 1955) Jerry Hopper
      In the Grand Canyon, the hero escapes from hostile
      Indians led by Delche (Pat Hogan).

549   Strange Lady in Town (Warner 1955) Mervyn LeRoy
      A female doctor from Boston works with Mexicans and
      Apaches, one of whom she cures of glaucoma.

550   The Tall Men (20th Cent-Fox 1955) Raoul Walsh
      The hero saves a woman during an Indian attack and
      later, when the Indians attack men on a cattle drive, he
      starts a stampede to turn them away.

551   The Vanishing American (Republic 1955) Joseph Kane
      In this remake of the 1925 film, Blandy (Scott Brady)
      is a Navajo who fights a crooked trader, Indian agent
      and hostile Apaches. As in the original, he loves a white
      woman who saves Yachi (Gloria Castillo), a young Indian
      woman, from the advances of a villain. Other Indian
      characters are Etenia (Julian Rivero), Coshonta (George
      Keymas), Quah-tain (Charles Stevens), and Beeteia (Jay
      Silverheels).

552   White Feather (20th Cent-Fox 1955) Robert Webb
      While the hero and Appearing Day (Debra Paget), an
      Indian woman he loves, try to stop a war between the
      cavalry and the Cheyenne Indians of the wise and peace-
      loving Chief Broken Hand (Eduard Franz); his son, Lit-
      tle Dog (Jeffrey Hunter), and his friend, American
      Horse (Hugh O'Brian), want to fight in order to save
      their honor. A NYT critic comments: "... the Red Man
      is not a marauding scoundrel. He is, instead, a truly
      brave warrior but somehow a sad figure, resigned, at
      last, to the truth that the White Man is strong enough to
      oust him from his hunting grounds and that he must
      move to new lands." (17 Feb 1)

553   Yellowneck (Republic 1955) R. John Hugh
      In the great swamp, hostile Seminoles threaten Con-
      federate deserters called "yellownecks."

1956

554 Around the World in 80 Days (UA 1956) Michael Anderson
     After the world travelers encounter peaceful Indians
who smoke the pipe with the engineer and do an orderly
circle dance in their idyllic village, hostile Sioux attack
the train, capture the hero's friend and are about to burn
him at the stake when the hero and the cavalry come to
the rescue.

555 Blazing the Overland Trail (Columbia 1956) Spencer Ben-
     net
     In the chapter of this serial entitled "Rifles for Red-
skins," the villain gets the Indians to attack a wagon
train.

556 Comanche (UA 1956) George Sherman
     Despite the efforts of Indian hating villains, the hero
persuades Quanah Parker (Kent Smith), Chief of the
Comanches, to sign a peace treaty. Flat Mouth (Mike
Mazurki) and Black Cloud (Henry Brandon) are Hostile
Comanches who defy the chief.

557 Dakota Incident (Republic 1956) Lewis K. Foster
     Sioux led by a chief (Charles Horvath) pin down a
small group of whites in a gully and eventually kill most
of them.

558 Daniel Boone, Trailblazer (Republic 1956) Albert Ganna-
     way, Ismael Rodriguez
     Indians threaten a wagon train led by the hero.

559 Ghost Town (UA 1956) Allen Miner
     Cheyennes led by Dull Knife (Ed Hashim) pin down a
small group of whites in a deserted town.

560 The Last Hunt (MGM 1956) Richard Brooks
     A vicious Indian-hating buffalo hunter who beats a
half-breed companion (Russ Tamblyn) and kills a young
Indian, Spotted Hand (Ed Lovehill) vies with his hunting
companion for an Indian woman (Debra Paget). An NYT
critic feels the film has a good message: "The equating
of Indian hating with lust for slaughter is morally good."
(1 Mar 2)

561   The Last Wagon (20th Cent-Fox 1956) Delmer Daves
        Apaches attack a wagon train and kill everyone ex-
      cept some young people and the hero, who grew up with
      the Comanches and lost his Indian wife and two sons.
      After some hand-to-hand combat with the Indians, he
      leads the survivors to safety.

562   The Lone Ranger (Warner 1956) Stuart Heisler
        The hero and his companion, Tonto (Jay Silverheels)
      bring to justice an evil rancher who is fomenting trouble
      between the Indians and the whites.   The Indians kidnap
      the villain's daughter but then show their honor by re-
      turning her to her mother.

563   Massacre (20th Cent-Fox 1956) Louis King
        Yaqui Indians, supplied with guns by smugglers, at-
      tack and kill a group of Mexicans.

564   Massacre at Sand Creek (Columbia 1956)
        In this Playhouse 90 television film, Colonel Chivington
      attacks unsuspecting and helpless Cheyenne women,
      children and elderly.

565   Mohawk (20th Cent-Fox 1956) Kurt Neumann
        After a villain joined by Pokhawah (Neville Brand)
      and hostile Mohawks start a war, against the wishes of
      Kowanen (Ted De Corsia) a wise and peaceful chief, and
      his wife Minikah (Mae Clarke), the hero comes to the res-
      cue and wins the hand of Onida (Rita Gam), a beautiful
      Indian woman.   A Variety reviewer notes that "Corsia and
      Clarke give dignity ... to their Indian characters."   (21
      Mar)

566   Perils of the Wilderness (Columbia 1956) Spencer Bennet
        In this serial, with chapters such as "Menace of the
      Medicine Man" and "Little Bear Pays a Debt," Indians
      are threats to the whites.

567   Pillars of the Sky (Universal 1956) George Marshall
        When Indians led by Chief Kamiakin (Michael Ansara)
      start a war because soldiers try to build a road and fort
      on land given to the Indians in a treaty, the death of a
      missionary living with the Indians stops the fighting.

568   Quincannon, Frontier Scout (UA 1956) Lesley Selander

A villain who has smuggled guns to the Indians of
Iron Wolf (Ed Hashim) and incited an attack on the whites,
is brought to justice by the hero.

569 Reprisal (Columbia 1956) George Sherman
     After two Indians have been unjustly hanged, the
half-breed hero (Guy Madison), at the urging of Taini
(Kathryn Grant) and a white woman sympathetic to the
Indians, takes on the villains and finally returns with
the white woman to his Indian people, two of whom are
Kakola (Philip Breedlove) and Kelene (Victor Zamudio).
A Newsweek critic comments: "The Indians, in line with
current Hollywood practice look pretty good. In fact,
if this new morality trend continues, moviegoers may
never see a bad Indian again." (19 Nov 135-6)

570 The Searchers (Warner 1956) John Ford
     The hero (John Wayne) and a young man, both of
whom have lost family members to the Comanches led by
Chief Scar (Henry Brandon), pursue two girls kidnapped
by the Indians. During their five-year search, the
young man accidentally acquires an Indian wife, Look
(Beulah Archuletta), who eventually disappears, and they
see women driven insane by the Indians. They eventually
find one of the girls, the hero's niece, and the young
man kills Chief Scar. The hero, after thinking about
killing his niece for having lived with an Indian, brings
her home with them. Other Indians in the film are
played by the following Indian actors, Away Luna, Billy
Yellow, Bob Many Mules, Exactly Sonnie Betsuie, Feather
Hat, Jr., Harry Black Horse, Jack Tin Horn, Many Mules
Son, Percy Shooting Star, Pete Grey Eyes, Pipe Line
Begishe, and Smile White Sheep. A Time reviewer refers
to them as "the same Navajo Indians who have been losing
battles in John Ford pictures since 1938." (25 June 60)

571 Secret of Treasure Mountain (Columbia 1956) Seymour
     Friedman
     Apaches, three of whom are Vahoe (Pat Hogan), Juan
Alvarado (Lance Fuller) and Tawana (Susan Cummings),
try to protect their gold from the villains.

572 Seventh Cavalry (Columbia 1956) Edmund Goulding
     Indians, one of whom is Young Hawk (Pat Hogan),
threaten soldiers trying to bury their dead after the Battle of Little Big Horn.

573 Walk the Proud Land (Universal 1956) Jesse Hibbs
     Also titled Apache Agent, this film deals with a his-
torical character, John Clum (Audie Murphy), an agent
of the San Carlos Apache reservation who takes care of
rebel Indians and finally brings peace to the reservation.
Tainay (Anne Bancroft), a beautiful Apache woman, offers her love to the hero but he remains faithful to his
wife. Other Indian characters are Geronimo (Jay Silverheels), Talito (Tommy Rall), Eskiminiyin (Robert Warwick), Tono (Eugene Mazzola), Alchise (Maurice Jara)
and Pica (Marty Carrizosa). A Time critic notes that the
film "is a western with a difference: the Indians, or
most of them, are the good guys." He goes on to write
that the hero "arrived with a novel idea, viz, that the
Apaches are human ... the kind of idea that makes him
unpopular with the local Army general, the state governor
and the boys in the corner saloon." (24 Sept 92)

574 White Squaw (Columbia 1956) Ray Nazarro
     When a villain tries to drive the Sioux and Ectay-O-
Wahnee (May Wynn), a half-breed woman living with them,
off their reservation, the hero comes to the rescue. At
the end the villain dies in a burning tepee.

575 Wild Dakotas (Assoc. Releasing 1956) Sam Newfield
     When a villain tries to cheat Araphoes out of their
land, the hero exposes the scheme and prevents a war.

576 Yaqui Drums (Allied Artists 1956) Jean Yarbrough
     A villain, trying to get land from the Yaqui, causes
trouble with the Indians.

                              1957

577 Apache Warrior (20th Cent-Fox 1957) Elmo Williams
     The Apache Kid (Keith Larsen), an Indian scout who
helps the hero hunt down the last Apache war parties,
goes to prison after he kills Chato (George Keymas), his
brother's murderer. After escaping from prison with the
help of rebel Apache Marteen (Rudolfo Acosta), and marrying Liwana (Eugenia Paul), he rejoins the hero to hunt
down the villains. Other Indian characters are Nantan
(John Miljan), an aged Apache Chief Chikisin (Dehl Berti),
and two Apache braves played by Eddie Little Sky and

Michael Carr. A Variety reviewer comments on the acting: "Larsen is becoming a specialist in Indian roles
(he's TV's 'Brave Eagle') and turns in a perceptive, well-
balanced portrayal.... As unreconstructed Apache menace, Acosta contributes convincing savagery." (24 July)

578 Copper Sky (20th Cent-Fox 1957) Charles Marquis Warren
     Apaches attack a town and kill all but the hero.

579 Deerslayer (20th Cent-Fox 1957) Kurt Neumann
     The Deerslayer (Lex Barker), reared by the Mohicans,
joins his blood brother, Chingachgook (Carlos Rivas) to
try to save an Indian-hating hunter and his daughters
from Hurons led by their chief (Joseph Vitale). The
film is loosely based on Cooper's novel.

580 Dragoon Wells Massacre (Allied Artists 1957) Harold
Schuster
     Hostile Apaches, led by a chief played by John War
Eagle, attack whites passing through their country.

581 Guns of Fort Petticoat (Columbia 1957) George Marshall
     The hero, who leaves the army because of his dis-
approval of the Sand Creek Massacre, trains a group of
women to fight Indians and they take on the Cheyenne,
led by a chief played by Charles Horvath, who are intent on revenge.

582 The Halliday Brand (UA 1957) Joseph H. Lewis
     The hero defends the right of his daughter to love
a half-breed, Jivaro (Christopher Dark).

583 Naked in the Sun (Allied Artists 1957) R. John Hugh
     Based on Frank Slaughter's The Warrior, this film
deals with a hero who battles Indian slavers during the
colonial period.

584 The Oklahoman (Allied Artists 1957) Francis D. Lyon
     Greedy ranchers try to frame Charlie Smith (Michael
Pate) an Indian rancher, to get his land. The hero,
whom Maria Smith (Gloria Talbott) an Indian servant
loves, comes to Smith's aid. An NYT critic praises the
film for offering "a hero who is man enough to make a
skin-conscious community ashamed of itself." (15 May
39)

585   Pawnee (Republic 1957) George Waggner
        Crazy Fox (Charles Horvath), a hostile brave who has
      taken control of Wise Eagle's (Ralph Moody) tribe, at-
      tacks a wagon train led by the hero who had grown up
      with the tribe. After killing Crazy Fox in hand-to-hand
      combat, the hero chooses a white woman in the wagon
      train rather than Dancing Fawn (Charlotte Austin), an
      Indian woman who loves him.

586   Quantez (Universal 1957) Harry Keller
        Apaches led by Delgadito (Michael Ansara) attack a
      gang of outlaws. A Variety critic notes that "Michael
      Ansara solidly repeats his video role (He's Indian Chief
      of 'Broken Arrow' series) as Apache leader." (28 Aug)

587   Revolt at Fort Laramie (UA 1957) Lesley Selander
        Red Cloud (Eddie Little Sky) and his Sioux attack a
      group of Confederate soldiers.

588   Ride Out for Revenge (UA 1957) Bernard Girard
        The hero rejects his own evil society and lives with
      Pretty Willow (Joanne Gilbert) and her Cheyenne tribe
      led by Yellow Wolf (Frank de Kova). They are all forced
      to live on an Oklahoma reservation despite the valiant re-
      sistance of Little Wolf (Vince Edwards).

589   Run of the Arrow (Universal 1957) Samuel Fuller
        A bitter Confederate soldier joins the Sioux and mar-
      ries Yellow Moccasin (Sarita Montiel) after he survives
      the painful "run of the arrow" test. After joining Walk-
      ing Coyote (Jay C. Flippen), Blue Buffalo (Charles Bron-
      son), Crazy Wolf (H.M. Wynant), Red Cloud (Frank de
      Kova) and Silent Tongue (Billy Miller) on some of their
      raids, he finally rejects the Indians because of their
      cruelty.

590   The Tomahawk Trail (UA 1957) Lesley Selander
        Captured by Apaches and befriended by Tula (Lisa
      Montell), the daughter of the chief, the heroine is final-
      ly rescued by some soldiers.

591   Trooper Hook (UA 1957) Charles Marquis Warren
        When Apache chief Nachez (Rudolfo Acosta) attacks a
      stagecoach carrying his white wife and their son, he is
      killed and she and the boy go off with the hero.

592 War Drums (UA 1957) Reginald LeBorg
     Villains push Mangas Coloradas (Lex Barker) and Riva
(Joan Taylor), his brave half-breed wife, into breaking
a treaty. The hero helps them escape an unjust punishment and go into the mountains with their Apache people,
some of whom are Chino (John Colicos), Nona (Jil Jar-
myn), Yellow Moon (Jeanne Carmen) and Delgadito (Ward
Ellis). A Variety critic comments that "Mangas Coloradas
... almost as durable a screen figure as Cochise ... is
an honorable Indian." (3 April)

593 Westward Ho the Wagons! (Buena Vista 1957) William
Beaudine
     Pawnees attack a wagon train. Hostile Sioux become
friendly after a doctor saves the life of Little Thunder
(Anthony Numkena) the son of the Sioux chief, Wolf's
Brother (John War Eagle). Many Stars (Iron Eyes Cody)
is a medicine man who fails to help the boy.

                          1958

594 Ambush at Cimarron Pass (20th Cent-Fox 1958) Jodie
Copelan
     Apaches attack and harass a small group of whites
until the hero finally brings the survivors to safety.

595 Apache Territory (Columbia 1958) Ray Nazarro
     Apaches, one of whom is Lugo (Frank De Kova),
threaten the hero who eventually uses dynamite to kill
them.

596 Blood Arrow (20th Cent-Fox 1958) Charles Marquis Warren
     When hostile Blackfoot led by Little Otter (Richard
Gilden) attack a Mormon woman bringing serum to some
sick families, some whites and an Indian, Taslatch (Rocky
Shahan), come to her rescue.

597 Bullwhip (Allied Artists 1958) Harmon Jones
     The hero tames his strong-willed half-breed wife,
Cheyenne (Rhonda Fleming).

598 Cowboy (Columbia 1958) Delmer Daves
     Indians, one of whom is Alcaide (Frank de Kova),
threaten some cattlemen.

599   Escape from Red Rock (20th Cent-Fox 1958) Edward
      Bernds
          After the hero and his woman find in a cabin a baby
      whose parents were killed by the Indians, Apaches at-
      tack them.

600   Fort Bowie (UA 1958) Howard W. Koch
          After soldiers kill a band of Apaches who were sur-
      rendering peacefully, the Apaches of Chief Victorio (Lar-
      ry Chance) attack and occupy a fort until Chenzana
      (Jana Davi), an Apache in love with the hero, helps the
      soldiers win it back. A Variety critic comments: "A
      switch is made from usual films of this category by having
      the cavalry storm their own fort after Indians have cap-
      tured it." (5 Feb)

601   Fort Dobbs (Warner 1958) Gordon Douglas
          Using a new repeating rifle, the hero defends the
      fort from a Comanche attack. A Variety critic notes
      that "there's no telling how many Comanches were done
      in by Walker (the hero) and his sharp-shooting friends,
      but after the fifth raid there was no contest." (22 Jan)

602   Fort Massacre (UA 1958) Joseph M. Newman
          An Indian-hating soldier whose wife and children were
      killed by Indians, tries to provoke an attack so he can
      get his revenge. Indian characters are a Paiute girl
      (Susan Cabot), Moving Cloud (Larry Chance), a Paiute
      man (Francis McDonald) and the chief (Walter Kray). A
      Variety critic comments that "Susan Cabot, as an Indian
      girl, is a beaut but no Paiute." (30 April)

603   Gun Fever (UA 1958) Mark Stevens
          The hero seeks his revenge after Indians led by the
      villain kill his parents. The Indian characters are Tanana
      (Jana Davi) who marries the good son of the villain and
      two chiefs (played by Iron Eyes Cody and Eddie Little
      Sky).

604   Gunman's Walk (Columbia 1958) Phil Karlson
          Clee Chonard (Kathryn Grant) is a half-breed Indian
      woman who suffers from racial prejudice. Another Indian
      character is Black Horse (Chief Blue Eagle). A Variety
      critic notes that the film has "contemporary pertinency
      with the outspoken discussion of racial elements, in this
      case, involving the Indians." (18 June)

605 The Law and Jake Wade (MGM 1958) John Sturges
     Comanche attack whites in a ghost town. A Time
critic describes them as "a tribe of cosmetic Comanches
who bite the dust as delicately as though it were crepes
suzette." (19 July 82)

606 The Light in the Forest (Buena Vista 1958) Herschel
Daugherty
     The Delaware of Cuyloga (Joseph Calleia) kidnap a
young white boy who is then named Young True Son
(James MacArthur). He lives with them until a treaty
forces them to send him back to his natural parents.
Unhappy with white society, especially when he meets an
Indian hater, the teenager finally learns to accept the
existence of good and bad people in each society after
he also sees treachery among the Indians. An NYT critic comments: "He [MacArthur] is saturnine and stiff....
But, of course, he is supposed to be acting a young
fellow raised up to Indian ways, which are notoriously
stolid and monosyllabic." (11 July 15)

607 The Lone Ranger and the Lost City of Gold (UA 1958)
Lesley Selander
     When villains try to gain control of an Indian mine,
the Lost City of Gold, the hero and Tonto (Jay Silverheels) thwart the plot and return the mine to the Indians,
three of whom are Chief Tomache (John Miljan), Redbird
(Maurice Jara) and Canlama (Belle Mitchell).

608 Oregon Passage (Allied Artists 1958) Paul Landres
     After Black Eagle (H.M. Wynant) a Shoshone chief,
kills whites whose ignorance of the Indians lead to their
deaths, the hero finally kills him in hand-to-hand combat
to stop an attack on the fort. Other Indian characters
are Little Deer (Toni Gerry) and Nato (Paul Fierro).

609 Tonka (Buena Vista 1958) Lewis R. Foster
     White Bull (Sal Mineo), a Sioux boy, trains the horse
Tonka, which is later sold to a cavalry officer and is
the only survivor after an arrogant and fanatical Custer
(Britt Lomond) leads his soldiers into the Battle of Little
Big Horn. Other Indian characters are Sitting Bull
(John War Eagle); Strong Bear (Rafael Campos), White
Bull's friend; Yellow Bull (H.M. Wynant), his enemy, and
Prairie Flower (Joy Page), his mother. A Variety critic

comments that the film "is probably somewhat romantic
in its view of the Sioux, but seeing the whole thing
through Indian eyes, and the eyes of an Indian youth,
at that, gives the story a fresh approach." (17 Dec)

1959

610 Escort West (UA 1959) Francis D. Lyon
     Modoc Indians (two of whom are played by Chuck
Howard and Charles Soldani) threaten the whites.

611 The FBI Story (Warner 1959) Mervyn LeRoy
     In one segment, the agents pursue murderers of
Osage Indians who own oil fields in Oklahoma.

612 Last Train from Gun Hill (Paramount 1959) John Sturges
     The hero hunts down two white men who raped and
killed his Indian wife.

613 Never So Few (MGM 1959) John Sturges
     In this World War II film, Sgt. John Danforth (Charles
Bronson) is a soldier who is an angry man because of
the way he's been treated as an Indian.

614 The Oregon Trail (20th Cent-Fox 1959) Gene Fowler
     Indians threaten a wagon train in a film which uses
the title of four previous westerns.

615 The Sheriff of Fractured Jaw (20th Cent-Fox 1959) Raoul
     Walsh
     In this spoof of westerns, the odd manners of the
English sheriff tame the Indians. In one part his awk-
ward horseback riding stops an attack and in another he
becomes the blood brother of Running Deer (Jonas Apple-
garth) and Red Wolf (Joe Buffalo).

616 Thunder in the Sun (Paramount 1959) Russell Rouse
     When Indians threaten a group of Basques, the for-
eigners, because of their knowledge of mountain terrain,
attack and defeat the Indians in their own country.

617 The Wonderful Country (UA 1959) Robert Parrish
     After Apaches kill some soldiers, the hero hunts them
down.

618 Yellowstone Kelly (Warner 1959) Gordon Douglas
      The hero, a friend of Gall (John Russell), the just
and honorable Chief of the Sioux, rescues Wahleeah
(Andra Martin) and kills the hostile Sagapi (Ray Danton).
Though Gall loves Wahleeah, he lets the hero take her
away.

                              1960

619 All the Young Men (Columbia 1960) Hall Bartlett
      In this film about the Korean War, an Indian soldier,
Hunter (Mario Alcalde), sides with the black hero because he has also known prejudice.

620 Comanche Station (Columbia 1960) Budd Boetticher
      After Comanches capture and rape a white woman,
the hero rescues her. The Indian characters are a
Comanche lance bearer (Foster Hood), chief (Joe Mo-
lina) and warrior (Vince St. Cyr).

621   Flaming Star (20th Cent-Fox 1960) Don Siegel
      Pacer Burton (Elvis Presley), the half-breed son of
Neddy Burton (Dolores Del Rio) a Kiowa Indian, is a
victim of prejudice from both sides. The hostile Kiowas
of Buffalo Horn (Rudolfo Acosta) kill his father and
the whites kill his mother. At the end he also sees the
"flaming star of death." Other Indian characters are
Ph'Sha Knay (Marian Goldina), Two Moons (Perry Lopez),
Bird's Wing (Sharon Bercutt), and an Indian brave
(Rodd Redwing). An NYT critic comments, "Indians are
not simply presented as 'heavies' but also as beleaguered
men being ruthlessly deprived, in their view, of their
lands." He concludes that the unhappy ending "seems
to underline the sadness of the period when the Indian
began to vanish." (17 Dec 19)

622 For the Love of Mike (20th Cent-Fox 1960) George Sherman
      Mike, a twelve-year-old Indian, wins a horse race
and gives the money to the Catholic Church. Other Indian characters are Tony Eagle (Armando Silvestre) and
Mrs. Eagle (Elsa Cardenas).

623 Geronimo's Revenge (Buena Vista 1960) James Neilson

This Disney movie is composed of episodes from the serial of Texas John Slaughter and the Apaches.

624 Oklahoma Territory (UA 1960) Edward L. Cahn
The hero has to prosecute his friend Buffalo Horn (Ted de Corsia), but then arranges for his escape and finally wins his acquittal. Buffalo Horn's daughter is Ruth Red Hawk (Gloria Talbott) and his son is Running Cloud (X. Brands). A Variety critic, commenting on the white actors, writes that Gloria Talbott looks "about as much like an Injun as Ted de Corsia, who doesn't." (10 Feb)

625 Savage Innocents (Paramount 1960) Nicholas Ray
Inuk (Anthony Quinn), a good-natured Eskimo, marries Asiak (Yoko Tani) and provides for his wife's family. Later, after he accidentally kills a missionary who doesn't understand his customs, two Mounties hunt him down. But the one Mountie Inuk rescues lets him go back to his family. A Newsweek critic comments: "As for the movie's message, it is that civilization should leave the morals of simple people alone; civilized people who have heard this a few times before will be pardoned for feeling that it also works the other way around." (27 Feb 1961, 91)

626 Sergeant Rutledge (Warner 1960) John Ford
In a series of flashbacks at the trial of a black cavalryman, the black hero is seen protecting a white woman from hostile Apaches, and then stopping the cavalry from riding into an ambush.

627 The Unforgiven (UA 1960) John Huston
Based on the novel by Alan Lee May, this film deals with the struggle of Rachel Zachary (Audrey Hepburn), a Kiowa raised by a white family who thought she was white. When her identity is revealed she suffers from the prejudice of the whites and the anger of the Indians, one of whom is Lost Bird (Carlos Rivas), who wants her back. In the Indian attack, she kills her own brother. A Saturday Review critic comments, "The film finds nothing wrong in the fact that a white family stole an Indian baby; because they gave it love and a good home, presumably, everything is fine. And the Indian girl is asked to express her gratitude by killing her brother." (16 April 32)

628 Walk Tall (20th Cent-Fox 1960) Maury Dexter
     With the help of Shoshone warriors, Chief Black Feath-
er (Felix Locher) and Buffalo Horn (Dave De Paul), the
hero stops an evil Indian killer whose attacks on the Indians could lead to war.

                              1961

629 All Hands on Deck (20th Cent-Fox 1961) Norman Taurog
     In this comedy, Shrieking Eagle (Buddy Hackett) is
a Chickasaw who wears a feather in his sailor hat. He
tears apart a theatre after seeing a cowboy and Indian
movie and he keeps threatening to scalp the admirals.

630 The Canadians (20th Cent-Fox 1961) Burt Kennedy
     When villains kill some Sioux and the survivors, two
of whom are the White Squaw (Teresa Stratas) and Chief
Four Horns (Michael Pate), seek revenge by driving them
off a cliff, the hero tries to restore peace.

631 Comancheros (20th Cent-Fox 1961) Michael Curtiz
     The heroes deal with the Comancheros, renegades who
supply the hostile Comanches of Iron Shirt (George
Lewis) with weapons and provisions. A New Yorker
critic comments: "In Hollywood, the only good Comanches
are dead Comanches.... Moreover, every bullet seeks
out a vital zone and promptly extinguishes its victim--
have you ever noticed in Westerns that white men can be
shot and wounded not once but many times, while Indians
who get shot almost always die instantly?" (9 Dec 235)

632 Frontier Uprising (Zenith 1961) Edward L. Cahn
     When the Modoc Indians of Chief Taztay (Herman Ru-
din) attack a wagon train and trap a troop of cavalry in
a canyon, the hero comes to the rescue.

633 The Outsider (Universal 1961) Delbert Mann
     This film tells the story of Ira Hayes (Tony Curtis)
one of the soldiers who raised the flag on Iwo Jima, from
the time he leaves his Pima reservation in Arizona until
he dies from alcoholism and exposure ten years later.
The death of Hayes' white friend, his inability to handle
the publicity of his heroism, and his own people's rejection of him lead to his alcoholism. Other Indian charac-

ters are Nancy Hayes (Vivian Nathan) his mother, and Jay Morago (Edmund Hashim), the chief of the tribe who befriends Hayes. An NYT critic comments: "One is conscious of a rare, honest, documentary-like treatment .... His laconic but obviously loving family are Arizona Indians, poor but proud of their heritage and hamstrung by governmental indifference to the lack of water for their parched acres." (8 Feb 25)

634 The Purple Hills (Assoc Producers 1961) Maury Dexter
     Apaches led by Chito (Danny Zapien) attack and kill the villain.

635 Thunder of Drums (MGM 1961) Joseph M. Newman
     Apaches attack two women living in a remote shed. A Variety critic refers to them as "a band of ornery neighborhood Apaches of the old screen school of all-bad Injuns." (30 Aug)

636 Two Rode Together (Columbia 1961) John Ford
     The cynical heroes bring back whites captured by the Comanches of Quanah Parker (Henry Brandon) years before. However, the ex-captives can't fit into white society: a young man named Running Wolf (David Kent) is lynched and a Mexican woman who had been raped by the Indians and taken as wife by Stone Calf (Woody Strode), a black man who struggles with Quanah Parker for power in the tribe, is rejected by the whites.

1962

637 Along the Mohawk Trail (ITC 1962) Sam Newfield, Sidney Salkow The Red Man and the Renegades; The Long Rifle and the Tomahawk; The Pathfinder
     Drawn from a television series based on Cooper's Last of the Mohicans, these TV movies deal with the adventures of Hawkeye (John Hart) and Chingachgook (Tom Chaney).

638 Geronimo (UA 1962) Arnold Laven
     After Geronimo (Chuck Connors) and his Apaches, three of whom are Delahay (Adam West), Huera (Enid Jaynes) and Nachez (Armando Silvestre), are manipulated by a villain, they flee to Mexico. They then go on raids

into the U.S., during which they take Teela (Kamala
Devi), the reservation teacher who eventually marries
Geronimo. When the raids get the attention of Washington, a Senator comes to set up a fair and just treaty.
A Variety critic comments: "The picture has an uplift
ending that may fool youngsters into concluding that the
Indian ultimately got a decent shake after all--a false
note of resolution contradicted by history to this day."
(25 Apr)

639 Requiem for a Heavyweight (Columbia 1962) Ralph Nelson
        Mountain Rivera (Anthony Quinn), an over-the-hill
     fighter who is part Indian, finally has to wear an Indian
     outfit to get a job as a wrestler. At the end, while the
     crowd laughs at his outfit, he does a war dance and
     waves his tomahawk at them.

640 Sergeants 3 (UA 1962) John Sturges
        The Indians of Mountain Hawk (Henry Silva) capture
     the three comic heroes but later they manage to save the
     cavalry from an ambush. Other Indian characters are
     Watanka (Michael Pate), White Eagle (Richard Hale) and
     Ghost Dancer (Eddie Little Sky). A Variety critic notes
     that "Henry Silva plays forcibly and believably as the
     baddest Indian on the premises." (24 Jan)

641 The Wild Westerners (Columbia 1962) Oscar Rudolph
        Sioux warriors, two of whom are Yellow Moon (Ilse
     Burkert) and Wasna (Hans Wedemeyer), attack the whites.

                              1963

642 How the West Was Won (MGM 1963) John Ford, George
     Marshall, Henry Hathaway
        In one part, the Indians stampede buffaloes in their
     attack on railroad builders.

643 Indian Paint (Eagle American 1963) Norman Foster
        In this all-Indian drama, Nishko (Johnny Crawford),
     the son of Hevatanu (Jay Silverheels), the Chief of the
     Arikara Indians, rescues his white stallion from the
     Comanches. After many adventures, he allows the horse
     to go free but it follows him as he returns to his people.
     Other Indian characters are Sutamakis (Pat Hogan),

Wacopi (Robert Crawford, Jr.), Nopawallo (George
Lewis), Amatula (Joan Hallmark), Sutako (Bill Blackwell),
Lataso (Al Doney) and Petala (Cinda Siler).

644   Kings of the Sun (UA 1963) J. Lee Thompson
         After Hunac Ceel (Leo Gordon) attacks the Mayans
      led by Balam (George Chakiris), the Mayans flee to the
      north where they then do battle with the Indians of
      Black Eagle (Yul Brynner). Balam saves the life of the
      captured Black Eagle who has fallen in love with Ixchel
      (Shirley A. Field), a woman betrothed to Balam, and the
      two tribes unite to triumph over Hunac Ceel. But Black
      Eagle is killed when he saves the life of his friend Balam
      during the battle. Other Indian characters are Ah Min
      (Richard Basehart), a high priest, Ah Haleb (Brad Dex-
      ter), Ah Yok (Barry Morse) and Isatai (Armando Silves-
      tre).

645   McLintock! (UA 1963) Andrew V. McLaglen
         Comanches just released from prison threaten a town.
      The Indian characters are Davey Elk (Perry Lopez),
      Puma (Michael Pate), and Running Buffalo (John Stanley),
      a friendly Comanche drunk. The hero (John Wayne)
      acts as a spokesman for the Comanche.

646   Savage Sam (Buena Vista 1963) Norman Tokar
         After the dog, Savage Sam, leads the heroes to some
      Apaches who have captured two children, there is a bat-
      tle with hostile Comanches. The Indian characters are
      a Comanche chief (Dean Fredericks), Broken Nose (Pat
      Hogan), Bandy Legs (Rudolfo Acosta) and a young war-
      rior (Rafael Campos) described by a Variety critic as
      "prominent in the hapless band of Indians whose inten-
      tions are never really clear and whose behavior is ex-
      tremely confusing." (22 May 1963)

647   Winnetou Part I (Columbia 1963) Harold Reinl, Stipe Delic
         Old Shatterhand (Lex Barker) and Winnetou (Pierre
      Brice), the Apache chief, overcome threats to their lives,
      become friends, and thwart the efforts of the villain who
      is after Apache gold. The film is based on Karl May's
      Winnetou, a novel immensely popular in Germany and
      Europe, but little known in the United States.

1964

648   Apache Rifles (20th Cent-Fox 1964) William Witney
      Villains after gold incite the Apaches of Red Hawk
      (Michael Dante) to attack. The Indian-hating hero, who
      changes his ways after falling in love with a half-breed,
      Dawn Gillis (Linda Lawson), comes to the rescue.

649   Blood on the Arrow (Allied Artists 1964) Sidney Salkow
      After Apaches, one of whom is Kai La (Robert Carri-
      cart), attack a trading post and kidnap a boy, the hero
      leads them into a trap and rescues the child.

650   Cheyenne Autumn (Warner 1964) John Ford
      Based on the historical novel of Mari Sandoz, this
      film depicts the heroic flight of the Cheyenne from Okla-
      homa to their homeland in the north. (See pages 82-85
      for a discussion of the film.)

651   A Distant Trumpet (Warner 1964) Raoul Walsh
      After the Chiricahua Apaches of Chief War Eagle have
      been driven into Mexico, the hero, whose life the chief
      saves, persuades the U.S. government to give the In-
      dians a reservation in Arizona. A Variety critic comments:
      "Hardly a white man bites the dust, yet the Redmen con-
      sistently get picked off like ducks at a shooting gallery.
      How one-sided can you get?" (27 May)

652   He Rides Tall (Universal 1964) R.G. Springsteen
      Hostile Indians kill and scalp a white woman.

653   Island of the Blue Dolphins (Universal 1964) James B.
      Clark
      A Chumash Indian girl, Karana (Celia Kaye), is aban-
      doned for almost twenty years on an island after evil
      trappers kill her father, Chowig (Carlos Romero). She
      survives numerous hardships and the loss of her brother,
      Ramo (Larry Domasin), before missionaries rescue her.

654   Navajo Run (American 1964) Johnny Seven
      A villain tricks Matthew Whitehawk (Johnny Seven),
      a half-breed Navajo, and leaves him in the woods. He
      then hunts him down as he has done before with other
      Indians. At the end Matthew kills him with a rattle-
      snake.

655   Pajama Party (American 1964) Don Weis
      Chief Rotten Eagle (Buster Keaton) helps some con
men crash the pajama party.

656   Rio Conchos (20th Cent-Fox 1964) Gordon Douglas
      The Indian-hating hero tries to stop villains who are
running guns to the Apaches led by the hostile Blood-
shirt (Rudolfo Acosta). After the Indians capture the
heroes and torture them by hitting them as they are
being dragged by horses, an Indian woman, Sally (Wende
Wagner), helps them escape.

657   Taggart (Universal 1964) R.G. Springsteen
      Hostile Apaches harass settlers. A Variety critic
notes that the film uses "every device in Western corral,
from cattle stampede straight through to lost gold mine,
and Indian attacks on wagon train and fort. Script is
traditional in the attitude towards Indians; only good
ones are dead ones." (9 Dec)

658   Winnetou II (Columbia 1964) Harold Reinl
      Also called Last of the Renegades, this German film
based on a Karl May novel deals with the exploits of
Old Shatterhand (Lex Barker) and Winnetou (Pierre
Brice), the Apache chief, as they stop villains who are
inciting the Indians to war.

659   Yanco (Jerand Film 1964) Servando Gonzalez
      In this Mexican film, a young Indian, Juanito (Richard
Ancona), who learns to play the violin, unintentionally
scares his people with his music and, as they chase him
at night, he drowns. A Saturday Review critic notes
that "the story takes place in a small Mexican Indian village still immersed in its ancient days." (11 July 23)

660   Young Guns of Texas (20th Cent-Fox 1964) Maury Dexter
      The hero, raised by Comanches, fights Apaches and
loves a woman who is prejudiced towards Indians.

                            1965

661   Arizona Raiders (Columbia 1965) William Witney
      The hero rescues Martina (Gloria Talbott), the daughter

of the Yaqui chief. A Variety critic comments: "A story
twist has a tribe of Yaqui Indians--for once pictured as
good guys, although they put the outlaws through some
exquisite Yaqui cactus torture--helping the star clean up
the gang." (21 July)

662 Cat Ballou (Columbia 1965) Elliot Silverstein
     Jackson Two-Bears (Tom Nardini), a Sioux bronc
buster, is a member of Cat's gang. A Newsweek critic
comments, "The Indian, though he speaks no Hebrew,
manages impeccable English and continually corrects other people's grammar. He even knows about the history
of art...." (10 May 118)

663 Deadwood '76 (Fairway 1965) James Landis
     Indians, one of whom is Spotted Snake (Gordon
Schwenk), capture the hero who then falls in love with
Little Bird (LaDonna Cottier) who is later raped by two
cowboys. When the hero gets his revenge by killing
them, a mob lynches him.

664 The Desert Raven (Allied Artists 1965) Alan S. Lee
     Raven (Rachel Romen), protected by her mother,
Rena (Bea Silvern), finally falls in love with a reformed
gangster whom she will marry when he gets out of prison.

665 Fort Courageous (20th Cent-Fox 1965) Lesley Selander
     Hostile Indians finally let a small group of soldiers
who have fought off many attacks leave the fort as a
show of respect for their courage.

666 Glory Guys (UA 1965) Arnold Laven
     The heroes battle hostile Sioux who have been killing
whites.

667 The Great Sioux Massacre (Columbia 1965) Sidney Salkow
     In this film about the Battle of Little Big Horn, Cus-
ter (Philip Carey), who is initially a friend to the Indians
and an enemy of crooked politicians and Indian agents,
finally agrees to mistreat the Indians for political reasons.
Sitting Bull (Michael Pate) and Crazy Horse (Iron Eyes
Cody) lead the Sioux against Custer.

668 The Hallelujah Trail (UA 1965) John Sturges
     In this spoof of westerns, Sioux, three of whom are

Elks Runner (Jim Burk), Chief Five Barrels (Robert
Wilke) and Chief Walks-Stooped Over (Martin Landau),
go after whiskey harassing a wagon train. In one scene
the Indians assume the traditional closed wagon formation
and the cavalry circles them. A Variety critic comments:
"One of the standouts in pic is Martin Landau, as Chief
Walks-Stooped Over, as deadpan as any Injun ever lived
but socking over his comedy scenes mostly with his eyes."
(16 June)

669 Major Dundee (Columbia 1965) Sam Peckinpah
        The hero and his soldiers pursue into Mexico the hos-
     tile Apaches of Sierra Charriba (Michael Pate) who have
     massacred whites and kidnapped three children. An NYT
     critic comments, "This particular West is an ugly place,
     and the director's camera searches intractably for its
     grimmest aspects. Indian murders are brutal and gory,
     the pillaged villagers are starving and haggard, the hard-
     traveling troopers are dirty, tired and miserable." (8
     April 45)

670 Treasure of Silver Lake (Columbia 1965) Harold Reinl
        In this German film based on a Karl May novel, Old
     Shatterhand (Lex Barker) and his blood brother, Win-
     netou (Pierre Brice), bring to justice some outlaws, with
     the aid of hostile Indians whom Winnetou wins over to
     their side.

671 War Party (20th Cent-Fox 1965) Lesley Selander
        After Comanches kill most of the men in a patrol,
     Nicoma (Laurie Mock) helps the survivors blow up the
     Indians' ammunition and is killed in the process. At the
     end the hero kills the Comanche chief.

                              1966

672 Apache Uprising (Paramount 1966) R.G. Springsteen
        Apaches led by their young chief (Abel Fernandez)
     release white captives in exchange for their Chief Antone
     (Paul Daniel), and then take revenge on the villain for
     his crimes against them.

673 Born Losers (American 1966) T.C. Frank (Tom Laughlin)
        Billy Jack (Tom Laughlin), a half-breed, rescues a
     woman from a vicious motorcycle gang.

674 The Devil's Mistress (Holiday 1966) Orville Wanzer
     Liah (Joan Stapleton), a half-breed, uses her magical
     powers to take revenge on three white men, two of whom
     had raped her.

675 Duel at Diablo (UA 1966) Ralph Nelson
     The Indian-hating hero rescues a white woman who
     has had a child with the son of the Apache chief and
     wants to stay with him. After her husband, who is real-
     ly the villain, rejects her and the child, the Apaches of
     Chata (John Hoyt) attack and punish him. Other Indian
     characters are Chata's wife (Dawn Little Sky) and Alchise
     (Eddie Little Sky). A Time critic comments that "the at-
     tacking Apaches tend to come across as more or less un-
     fortunate bystanders.... If anything, Diablo proves
     that it can be extremely difficult to promote racial har-
     mony while playing cowboys-and-Indians." (1 July 78)

676 The Exiles (Pathé 1966) Kent MacKenzie
     Three young Indians leave their reservation and go
     to Los Angeles. After they realize they don't fit in the
     city, they go to a hilltop near the freeway and, in a fu-
     tile gesture, beat the drum and try to sing and dance in
     the traditional ways.

677 40 Guns to Apache Pass (Columbia 1966) William Witney
     After a hostile Cochise (Michael Keep) and his Apaches
     make all-out war, the hero struggles to keep them from
     getting new repeating rifles.

678 Frontier Hellcat (Columbia 1966) Alfred Vohrer and Stipe
     Delic
     In this German film based on a Karl May novel, Old
     Surehand (Stewart Granger) and his blood brother, Win-
     netou (Pierre Brice), with the help of the Shoshone,
     rescue a wagon train from the Vultures, who are villains
     disguised as Indians.

679 Johnny Reno (Paramount 1966) R.G. Springsteen
     When Chief Little Bear (Paul Daniel) finds out that
     his son has been killed for loving a white woman, his
     tribe attacks the town and takes revenge on the killer.

680 Johnny Tiger (Universal 1966) Paul Wendkos
     Johnny Tiger (Chad Everett), a half-breed Seminole

and the grandson of Chief Sam Tiger (Ford Rainey), is caught between a white teacher who wants him to educate himself so he can teach his people, and his grandfather who wants him to be a traditional Indian. Johnny marries the daughter of the teacher and promises to use his knowledge to help his people as their new chief. A Saturday Review feels that the film, "... although it deals with an Indian minority in present-day America, winds up curiously dated and even reactionary." (14 May 50)

681   Kid Rodelo (Paramount 1966) Richard Carlson
        Cavalry Hat (Jose Villa Sante), a Yaqui chief, pursues the hero who finally kills him.

682   Nevada Smith (Paramount 1966) Henry Hathaway
        The hero (Steve McQueen), a half-breed, is aided by Neesa (Janet Margolin), a Kiowa prostitute, in his attempt to revenge the killing of his father and Indian mother. A Newsweek critic notes that Neesa is played by an actress in "a deerskin suit and a New York accent." (11 July 90)

683   The Plainsman (Universal 1966) David Lowell Rich
        Cheyenne, supplied with repeating rifles by the villain and led by Crazy Knife (Henry Silva), capture Wild Bill Hickok (Don Murray) and Buffalo Bill (Guy Stockwell), but Black Kettle (Simon Oakland) comes to their rescue. A Time critic points out the clichés of "the noble old Indian chief [Black Kettle] 'Cheyenne not want war' and the nasty young brave [Crazy Knife] 'Kill! Kill!'." (9 Dec 111)

684   Rampage at Apache Wells (Columbia 1966) Harold Philipps
        In this German film based on a Karl May novel, Shatterhand and Winnetou (Pierre Brice) bring oil swindlers who incited Navajos to attack a wagon train by killing the chief's son to justice.

685   Run Appaloosa Run (Buena Vista 1966) Larry Lansburgh
        In this Disney film, Mary Blackfeather (Adele Palacios), the finest rider of her Nez Percé tribe, wins a big race on her horse, Holy Smoke. An NYT critic comments: "Added are some picturesque glimpses of Indians in tribal regalia, contrasted with dungaree-clad Indian youngsters

bouncing around in jeeps. Even the slight self-
consciousness of the performers ... adds a kind of
homespun luster." (14 July 78)

686   Stagecoach (20th Cent-Fox 1966) Gordon Douglas
      In this remake of the 1939 John Ford classic, Sioux
attack and great numbers of them are killed. An NYT
critic comments: "The attack on the stagecoach fills the
screen with whooping Indians, arrows and gunfire. And
a fiery finish that should warm the cockles of an arson-
ist's heart." (16 June 53)

687   The Talisman (Gillman 1966) John Carr
      After Cheyenne have attacked a wagon train, one of
them (Ned Romero) cares for and falls in love with the
white woman who is the only survivor. After three white
men rape the woman, the Indian gets his revenge by
killing each of them in a violent way: one is buried in
sand with ants and honey, one is torn apart by two bent
trees, and one is poisoned by a rattlesnake. A Variety
critic notes that the director tried for a certain look in
the Indian character: "a face that was primitive, brutal,
but not unattractive, proud, warlike, and definitely mascu-
line." (9 Oct 1968)

688   The Tall Women (Allied Artists 1966) Sidney Pink
      Apaches led by Pope (Luis Prendes) kill all but seven
women in a wagon train and then all the members of a
rescue squad except the hero. At the end Chief White
Cloud (Fernando Hilbeck) recognizes the courage of the
white survivors and orders Pope not to attack them again.

689   Texas Across the River (Universal 1966) Michael Gordon
      In this spoof of western stereotypes, the hero rescues
Lonetta (Tina Marquand), an Indian woman, from a
Comanche medicine man (Richard Farnsworth) and even-
tually falls in love with her. Other Indian characters
are Comanche Chief Iron Jacket (Michael Ansara), Yellow
Knife (Linden Chiles) his bumbling son, and Kronk (Joey
Bishop), the hero's wisecracking Indian companion. A
Time critic comments, "Director Michael Gordon (Pillow
Talk) has even more fun with the studio Indians, who
under their Redman-Tan look suspiciously as if they be-
longed to one of the Lost Tribes of Israel. They're a
sad lot." (9 Dec 111)

690   Winnetou III (Columbia 1966) Harold Reinl
    Also titled The Desperado Trail, this German film is
based on a Karl May novel. After a villain frames Winnetou (Pierre Brice), the Apache chief dies in a battle
with the villain and his renegade Indians. Valiantly he
steps in front of his blood brother Old Shatterhand and
takes a bullet meant for him. A Variety critic notes
that the film shows the heroes "riding and fighting together versus vicious pale faces and ill-guided Indians.
Winnetou knows that the white men and redskins could
live peacefully together if there weren't those unscrupulous white settlers who try to squeeze the Indians out of
their territory." (19 Jan)

                              1967

691   Africa--Texas Style (Paramount 1967) Andrew Marton
    John Henry (Tom Nardini) is the Navajo companion of
the hero who ends up driving a school bus in Africa.

692   Chuka (Paramount 1967) Gordon Douglas
    Although the hero aids Hanu (Marco Antonio) Chief
of the Arapahoe, the starving Indians later kill everyone
in the fort, helped by an Indian woman from within.

693   Custer of the West (Cinerama 1967) Robert Siodmak
    Custer (Robert Shaw) and his men attack and mas-
sacre an Indian encampment for the sake of politicians.
But he later fights for proper treatment of the Indians,
until his death at the Battle of Little Big Horn to the Indians under Chief Dull Knife (Kieron Moore). An NYT
critic notes that there are "signs that somebody meant to
try something fairly ambitious, to show the Indian Wars
through a contemporary sensibility, Custer as a thoroughly
modern man who would have liked Camus." (4 July 13)

694   Death Curse of Tartu (Thunderbird 1967) William Grefe
    Tartu (Doug Hobart), a Seminole witch doctor dead
for 400 years, comes back to kill some students who have
tampered with his grave.

695   Hondo and the Apaches (MGM 1967) Lee H. Katzin
    In this TV movie remake of Hondo, the hero deals with
the Apaches of Vittorio (Michael Pate).

696   Fort Utah (Paramount 1967) Lesley Selander
      Indians attack a stagecoach and the fort after a vil-
lain kills Indian women and children, but they stop when
the body of the villain is handed over to them. A Time
critic, referring to an ambush scene in which an Indian
jumps down from the rocks onto a lone rider, comments:
"The scene, portrayed for what must be the millionth
time, begins this assembly-line film, which includes almost every other cliché known to Western man." (26 May
94)

697   The Hellbenders (Embassy 1967) Sergio Corbucci
      In this Italian film, the Indians and their Chief
(Claudio Scarchilli) demand vengeance after a white man
tries to rape an Indian woman.

698   Hombre (20th Cent-Fox 1967) Martin Ritt
      A white man raised by the Apache (Paul Newman)
deals with racial prejudice as he fights an evil Indian
agent and other whites who have stolen Indian funds.
At the end Hombre gives his life to save the survivors
from the stagecoach. A Variety critic writes that the
film is "a conscious social commentary on greed, nobility,
prejudice and resignation." (15 Mar) An NYT critic notes
that Hombre's death is "mindful of the selfless sacrifices
made by the Indian hero in Broken Arrow." (22 Mar 41)

699   The Legend of Custer (Fox 1967) Norman Foster
      This TV movie deals with Custer (Wayne Maunder) as
Indian fighter.

700   The Legend of the Boy and the Eagle (Buena Vista 1967)
Jack Couffer
      This Disney film recreates the Hopi Legend of the
Eagle.

701   Navajo Joe (UA 1967) Sergio Corbucci
      In this Italian film, Navajo Joe (Burt Reynolds) takes
harsh revenge on the outlaws who killed everyone in his
village. In the process, he rescues an Indian woman,
Estella (Nicoletta Machiavelli) and saves a town besieged
by the outlaws.

702   Red Tomahawk (Paramount 1967) R.G. Springsteen
      After the Battle of Little Big Horn, the hero saves a

town from a Sioux attack. A <u>Variety</u> critic comments:
"'Red Tomahawk' reverts to the traditional western attitude towards women. Joan Caulfield is only slightly
tarnished and then, it's blamed on the Indians." (11
Jan)

703 <u>Shatterhand</u> (Goldstone 1967) Hugo Fregonese
        In this German film based on characters of Karl May,
     whites and renegade Comanches after Apache land make
     trouble for Winnetou (Pierre Brice) and his tribe. When
     Shatterhand (Lex Barker) is held prisoner in a fort, Win-
     netou comes to the rescue and in the battle his son, Tu-
     junga (Alain Tissier) is killed.

704 <u>The War Wagon</u> (Universal 1967) Burt Kennedy
        Levi Walking Bear (Howard Keel), an Indian rene-
     gade, is one of the hero's crew. Starving Kiowas led
     by Wild Horse (Marco Antonio) help the hero stop the
     war wagon but later attack to get the gold in the wagon.

705 <u>The Way West</u> (UA 1967) Andrew V. McLaglen
        After the son of the Sioux chief (Michael Lane) is
     killed, the hero has to hang the killer in order to stop
     an attack. Eddie Little Sky and Michael Keep play Sioux
     warriors.

706 <u>Welcome to Hard Times</u> (MGM 1967) Burt Kennedy
        John Bear (Royal Dano), a Pawnee, is one of four
     people who try to rebuild a town after it is terrorized
     by a villain.

1968

707 <u>Arizona Bushwackers</u> (Paramount 1968) Lesley Selander
        Apaches, supplied with rifles by the villain, attack a
     town.

708 <u>Day of the Evil Gun</u> (MGM 1968) Jerry Thorpe
        Apaches kidnap the hero's family and then attack a
     town.

709 <u>Flaming Frontier</u> (Warner 1968) Alfred Vohrer
        In this German film based on a Karl May novel, Sure-
     hand and his blood brother, the Apache chief Winnetou

(Pierre Brice) deal with Comanches angered by the murder of the chief's son.

710   The Hooked Generation (Allied Artists 1968) William Grefe
      Drug dealers hide out in a Seminole Indian camp and one of them rapes a young Indian woman.

711   The Savage Seven (American Inter. 1968) Richard Rush
      When business men and a motorcycle gang victimize Indians living in a California shanty town, Johnnie Littlehawk (Robert Walker, Jr.) fights back and defends his sister from the gang. After the rape of an Indian woman the bikers and the Indians, two of whom are Grey Wolf (Max Julien) and Running Buck (John Cardos), start killing each other.

712   The Scalphunters (UA 1968) S. Pollack
      After Kiowas led by Chief Two Crows (Armando Silvestre) take the furs of the hero and hand over a slave they have captured, the villains attack and kill all of the Indians but the chief. Later the Indians get their revenge on the villains and spare only the heroes and a white woman.

713   Shakiest Gun in the West (Universal 1968) Alan Rafkin
      In this remake of The Paleface (1947), after the Sioux led by a chief (Dick Wilson) attack, the comic hero disguises himself as a Indian woman to rescue his beloved, who is much more adept at fighting Indians than he is.

714   Shalako (Cinerama 1968) Edward Dymtryk
      Apaches attack Europeans hunting on Indian land. The hero comes to the rescue by freeing a female captive and winning a hand-to-hand fight with Chato (Woody Strode), the Apache chief. Another Indian character is Chato's father (Rodd Redwing).

715   The Stalking Moon (National 1968) Robert Mulligan
      When the hero decides to protect a white woman and her half-breed son (Noland Clay) from the Apache renegade Salvaje (Nathaniel Narcisco), the Indian kills the Indian friend of the hero, Nick Tana (Robert Forster), before the hero kills him. A Variety critic comments on this film based on the novel by Theodore V. Olsen:

"Salvaje never is developed so as to project the terror
force he is supposed to be. Instead he is little more
than a savage Indian." (18 Dec)

716 Stay Away Joe (MGM 1968) Peter Tewksbury
     In this comedy based on the novel by Dan Cushman,
Joe Lightcloud (Elvis Presley), a half-breed Navajo rodeo
champion, saves the day for his tribe after they use a
prize stud bull for a barbecue and his sister sells her
father's cattle. Both Joe and his sister, Mary (Katy
Jurado), are in love with whites. A Variety critic comments: "The basic story--contemporary American Indians who are portrayed as laughable incompetents--is out
of touch with latterday appreciation of some basic dignity
in all human beings.... Custer himself might be embar-
rassed--for the Indians." (13 Mar)

717 Three Guns for Texas (Universal 1968) David Lowell Rich,
     Paul Stanley, and Earl Bellamy
     Texas Rangers deal with Indians led by Linda Little
Trees (Shelley Morrison), who falls in love with one of
them. Later the Indians and the Rangers join forces to
fight the outlaws.

718 Where Angels Go ... Trouble Follows! (Columbia 1968)
     James Neilson
     In this comedy, Indian actors who are angry at the
filmmaker who employed them harass the heroines (nuns)
and a group of girls.

                          1969

719 Castle Keep (Columbia 1969) S. Pollack
     Private Henry Three Ears of an Elk (James Patterson)
is in the group of soldiers defending the castle in this
World War II film.

720 Hang Your Hat on the Wind (Buena Vista 1969) Larry
     Landsburgh
     In this Disney film a Navajo boy named Goyo (Ric
Natoli) finds a valuable escaped racehorse and names him
Tom Tom. Later the boy shows his honor by giving the
horse back to the owner.

721 Heaven with a Gun (MGM 1969) Lee H. Katzin
        The hero protects a young Indian woman, Leloopa
     (Barbara Hershey), and punishes the man who assaulted
     her.

722 MacKenna's Gold (Columbia 1969) J. Lee Thompson and
     Tom Shaw
        As the hero searches for gold in a valley sacred to
     the Apache, Hesh Ke (Julie Newmar), an Apache woman
     who is accompanied by the taciturn Hachita (Ted Cas-
     sidy), competes with a white woman for his affection.
     At the end after the Apaches attack, only the hero and
     the white woman escape.

723 Once upon a Time in the West (Paramount 1969) Sergio
     Leone
        Cheyenne (Jason Robards), a half-breed wrongly
     accused of a crime, gets his revenge.

724 100 Rifles (20th Cent-Fox 1969) Tom Gries
        Yaqui Joe (Burt Reynolds) is a half-breed who gets
     rifles for the Yaqui Indians led by Sarita (Raquel Welch).

725 The Ramrodder (Entertainment Ventures 1969) Van Guy-
     loler
        After a white man rapes an Indian woman and the In-
     dians (led by a chief played by Brave Eagle) retaliate
     by raping a white woman, the hero stops a war by hand-
     ing over the man to the Indians who then castrate him.
     At the end the hero marries Princess Tuwana (Kathy
     Williams), an Indian woman.

726 Satan's Sadists (Independent 1969) Al Adamson
        Firewater (John Cardos), who is the Indian friend of
     the sadistic leader of a motorcycle gang, finally rebels
     against him.

727 Smith! (Buena Vista 1969) Michael O'Herlihy
        In this Disney film, when Gabriel Jimmyboy (Frank
     Ramirez) a Nez Percé, is wrongly accused of murder, Ol
     Antoine (Chief Dan George) replaces Walter Charlie (War-
     ren Oates), a crooked Indian against the boy, and proves
     his innocence at the trial. A Variety critic comments,
     "Hollywood's Indian Actors Workshop, under direction of
     Jay Silverheels (who has small but winning role in court-

room), supplements regional feeling of film." (26 Mar)
However a critic from Holiday finds the portrayal of Indians offensive: "The movie insults Indians by portray-
ing them as childlike, simple-minded creatures incapable
of taking care of even their most basic needs.... Somebody should teach Indians how to sue." (June, 23)

728 Tell Them Willie Boy Is Here (Universal 1969) Abraham
Polonsky
     Based on Willie Boy, A Desert Manhunt by Harry Law-
ton, the film deals with the escape attempt of Willie Boy
(Robert Blake) a Paiute, and his beloved Lola (Katharine
Ross), whose father Willie accidentally kills. Pursued by
a sympathetic white sheriff and an Indian-hating posse
and aided by a liberal but misguided female Indian agent,
the two finally die in the desert. A Variety critic comments: "The social, sexual and economic conditions in
America--with Freudian and Marxian theories of human
motivations fully developed--which eventually makes Coop
[the sheriff] kill a deliberately unarmed Willie (thus, in
a sense, repeating the whole white-Indian history in
America) is what the film is all about." (22 Oct)

729 Undefeated (20th Cent-Fox 1969) Andrew McLaglen
     Some Cheyenne aid the hero, whose adopted son, Blue
Boy (Roman Gabriel), is from their tribe.

FILMS OF THE 1970s AND 1980s

Commenting on Journey Through Rosebud (1972), a Newsweek critic notes that "Recent literature and films have discovered the Indians' humanity" and are "trying to make amends," but, in the process, "white guilt ... pours forth enough tears to wash away the wigwam" (24 April 1972, 89). During this contemporary period a few films--such as Little Big Man (1970), House Made of Dawn (1972), and Spirit of the Wind (1982)-- finally get beyond such excessive sympathy for Indians. Although Little Big Man emphasizes the guilt and madness of white culture in its depiction of Merriwether, Hickok and Custer, it also marks a transition in its sympathetic picture of Cheyenne life, specifically with the character of Old Lodge Skins, who is given a unique humor and dignity by an Indian actor, Chief Dan George. In fact, the use of Indian actors for major roles is the critical element in the movement to films like House Made of Dawn and Spirit of the Wind, which show a new empathy for contemporary Indian characters who have significance in and of themselves, not as objects of pity or guilt.

Little Big Man is a useful transition to these new Indian films because, though sympathetic to the Indian characters, it still uses them only as political symbols to criticize contemporary values. Besides depicting traditional heroes like Wild Bill Hickok and Custer as mentally unbalanced, humorously desperate characters, the film criticizes the mentality behind white exploitation of other races by suggesting that the Washita massacre and the Battle of Little Big Horn are happening all over again in Vietnam. The two characters that the filmmaker, Arthur Penn, uses to get at this mentality are Allardyce T. Merriwether, a character more important in the film than his counterpart in the novel, and Old Lodge Skins, the old Chief of the Cheyenne and the hero's surrogate father.

Merriwether, the "snake oil" salesman who keeps losing

parts of his body, is the deep cynic who believes that all humans are fools and none of what they do really matters. He tries to convince the hero that he should take as much from others as he can get away with because there is no morality in the universe. Old Lodge Skins, on the other hand, believes that all life has a moral center and that everything in the world is alive and connected. For example, when the hero asks him why the soldiers killed Indian women and children, he replies, "Because they are strange; they don't know where the center is," and then later, referring again to an attack on an Indian camp, he says, "Indians believe everything is alive. That is the difference; for the white man everything is dead." At the end of the film Old Lodge Skins wants to die because he realizes that though his people beat Custer, they will not win the next battles and "a world without human beings [the Cheyenne] has no center." Only the amoral world of Merriwether, and, by implication, Vietnam, will exist.

Throughout the film, the director uses the values of Old Lodge Skins to make his point about white exploitation but he allows the actor to make the character more than a mouthpiece. For example, after Old Lodge Skins goes through his death ceremony and then doesn't die, his response, "Sometimes the magic works; sometimes it doesn't," is typical of the humor which Chief Dan George brings to the role. Another example occurs when he asks Little Big Man about his white wife, "Does she show pleasant enthusiasm when you mount her? I've never noticed it in a white woman." Frequently seen in low angle and close-up shots which emphasize his importance, Dan George delivers such lines in an understated way, but always with a unique twinkle in his eye. Although his character reflects the typical image of the wise old chief who knows the whites will eventually destroy the Indian way of life, the charming quirks that Dan George brings to the character make Old Lodge Skins the most human and dignified Indian of the westerns.

Indian actors bring the same quality to House Made of Dawn, a film based on the N. Scott Momaday novel which deals with contemporary Indians in a non-western setting. Though the film uses a complex pattern of flashbacks and imagery to suggest the stream of consciousness form of the novel, the real emotional center is the acting of Larry Littlebird as Abel and Jay Varela (a part Indian and deeply empa-

thetic actor) as his friend Ben. The contrast between these
characters reveals the dilemma of the modern Indian and the
dialogue and acting provide a restrained but powerful impact.
Abel dreams about returning to the land of his grandfather,
but Ben has no desire to return to the reservation which for
him is a place where "it's just a bunch of old people dying."
Later, after a policeman harasses and takes money from the
two men, Abel is defiant whereas Ben, who is used to taking
such treatment in order to survive in the city, only laughs
and suggests that, like with the cowboys and Indians, maybe
they could scalp him. Towards the end, after Abel stands
up to the policeman, takes a terrible beating, and finally decides to go home, he and Ben say goodbye at a bus depot in
a scene which brings the contrast between them to a touching
climax. As the filmmaker cuts between each character in close-
up shots, the actors, barely holding back tears, speak to
each other slowly and quietly. Abel asks, "What's it going
to be like?" and Ben, after a long pause, and knowing that
what he says will never happen, replies, "Sometime we'll meet
out there real early in the morning. We'll get drunk, sing,
see how it looks." The scene ends with a cut to a close-up
of Abel, whose eyes show his realization that he will never
see his friend again. His departure is a strong image of
the separation between the traditional and the urban Indian
but the real power of the scene comes from the restraint and
feeling that the actors bring to their roles.

Indian actors impart a similar feeling in Spirit of the
Wind, drawn from the real-life story of George Attla, the
Alaskan Indian who overcomes tuberculosis to become a
champion dogsled racer. Although other films deal with modern
Indian heroes--such as Jim Thorpe (Jim Thorpe All American,
1951), Ira Hayes (The Outsider, 1961), or Billy Mills (Running
Brave, 1983)--this one stands out because Indian actors play
all the main roles. A Variety critic notes, "There is a disarming quality to this film. It has a dedicated father with
patriarchal dignity and natural wisdom as well as the old
storyteller played with zest by Chief Dan George already known
from Little Big Man and other films" (23 May 1979). George
Clutesi infuses dignity into the character of the father with
his restrained delivery of wise and humorous lines. For instance, after he catches his hand in a trap, he says to George,
"I've been catching animals all my life; it's only fair I catch
myself once." Later, when George is dealing with the crafty
old Indian, Moses, his father says, "You've got to go easy on

George, he's been around white men too long." Chief Dan
George brings his characteristic humor to the character of
Moses, when, after George wins the big race with a lead dog
he got from the old man, he says with a dry delivery, "I
knew I should have kept that dog." All the Indian actors,
including George Attla (Pius Savage) and his mother (Rose
Attla Ambrose), look their parts and interact with a low-key,
good-natured respect for each other that gives the film its
"disarming quality." This ambience, along with Buffy St.
Marie's singing during the racing and transitional scenes,
gives the film a sense of being uniquely Indian, a true picture
of a different culture.

In both House Made of Dawn and Spirit of the Wind the
main characters find meaning within themselves and their traditional culture. When Abel returns to the land of his Indian
grandfather, he participates in the ceremony of the run, described by the old man, "It is a holy thing I believe. You
must believe it too. Those who run are the life that flows in
our people." Seen from an extreme low angle as he runs towards the sun, Abel finds a way to express himself and feel
his power through a traditional ceremony. Likewise, George
Attla becomes a champion only when he returns to the land and
learns about dog racing from Moses and his father. Each
character is a complicated and heroic Indian whose significance
does not really depend on a comparison or contrast to white
society, as is the case with the Indians in Little Big Man and
other westerns. The filmmakers don't use them for some other
purpose like instilling guilt; they empathize with them and
show respect for the uniqueness of American Indian culture.

1970

730 Big Beaver (Stacey Dist. 1970) Semore Lavender
       In this erotic film, Toronto (Mac Henry) and his
       woman, Head Piece (Thelma Handy), rape Blue Moon
       (Mary Thackery) during a battle between two tribes.
       Another example of such films with Indian characters is
       Kate and the Indians (1981), in which the Indians try
       to rape a white woman.

731 Cry Blood, Apache (Golden Eagle 1970) Jack Starrett
       When Apaches refuse to give the location of a gold

mine, whites kill all of them except Jemme (Marie Gahva)
and her brother, Vittorio (Don Kemp). After Vittorio
hunts down and kills most of the whites, Jemme kills him
to save the life of the hero, whom she loves.

732 Dirty Dingus Magee (MGM 1970) Burt Kennedy
     Anna Hotwater (Michele Carey), whom Chief Crazy
Blanket (Paul Fix) wants as his woman, is the comic
hero's lover who helps him escape the sheriff. Old Indian women are played by Mae Old Coyote, Lillian Hogan,
Florence Real Bird, and Ina Bad Bear.

733 El Condor (National General 1970) John Guillermin
     Renegade Apaches led by Santana (Iron Eyes Cody)
help the villain, who later kills the chief.

734 Flap (Warner 1970) Carol Reed
     In this film which is also titled The Last Warrior and
is based on Clair Huffaker's novel Nobody Loves a Drunk-
en Indian, Flapping Eagle (Anthony Quinn) is a hard-
drinking Indian war hero who, along with his friends
Lobo Jackson (Claude Akins) and Eleven Snowflake (Tony
Bill), battles a construction company, steals a train and
tries to claim the town for his tribe. Aided by Wounded
Bear Smith (Victor Jory) a self-styled Indian lawyer,
opposed by the Indian storekeep (Rudolfo Acosta) and
loved by Bluebell, a white prostitute, he finally is shot
by his enemy, Rafferty (Victor French), a brutal half-
breed policeman. Other Indian characters are Ann Looking Deer (Susana Miranda), Larry Standing Elk (Rudy
Diaz), She'll-Be-Back-Pretty-Soon (Pedro Regas) and
Luke Wolf (John War Eagle).
     A Variety critic comments: "There is no attempt to
show any Indian as a responsible person; instead, the
racial awakening seems rooted in nothing more than an
alcoholic feeling of "everyone-else-is-doing-it, why-not
us?" Those unfamiliar with Indian problems are likely
to be embarrassed for real Indians." (28 Oct)

735 Geronimo Jones (Learning Corp. 1970) Bert Salzman
     In this short film, a young Indian gets caught be-
tween the values of the past and present when he trades
an old medallion for a TV.

736 King of the Grizzlies (Buena Vista 1970) Ron Kelly

Moki (John Yesno), a Cree Indian, protects his white
boss from a grizzly bear that he cared for as a cub and
with whom he still feels a mystical connection.

737 Land Raiders (Columbia 1970) Nathan Juran
     After the Indian-hating villain incites Apaches to war
in order to decrease land values and then frames them
for the killing of an Indian agent, they retaliate by attacking a stagecoach. Then after the whites retaliate
by killing Indian women and children in a village, the
Apaches attack the town.

738 Little Big Man (National General 1970) Arthur Penn
     In this film based on Thomas Berger's novel, Jack
Crabb (Dustin Hoffman) is adopted by the Cheyenne of
Old Lodge Skins (Chief Dan George) and is in the Washita massacre and the Battle of Little Big Horn with
Custer (Richard Mulligan) who is portrayed as an ego-
maniac. (See pages 140-43 for further discussion of this
film.) Other Indian characters are Sunshine (Amy Ec-
cles), Little Big Man's wife; Little Horse (Robert Little
Star); Younger Bear (Cal Bellini); Shadow That Comes
in Sight (Ruben Moreno); and Burns Red in the Sun
(Steve Shemayne).

739 A Man Called Horse (National General 1970) Elliot Silver-
     stein
     The Sioux of Yellow Hand (Manu Tupou) kill every-
one in a hunting party but Lord John Morgan (Richard
Harris). They take the Englishman, name him Horse and
give him to an old woman, Buffalo Cow Head (Judith
Anderson). Though treated harshly, he decides to learn
the Sioux language and after proving himself as a warrior
by killing hostile Shoshone, he falls in love with Running
Deer (Corinna Tsopei) and undergoes the torture of the
Sun Vow to win her hand. After the Shoshone kill the
chief and his wife, Horse becomes the new chief but
leaves for England when Buffalo Cow Head dies. Other
Indian characters are Black Eagle (Eddie Little Sky),
Thorn Rose (Lina Marin), Elk Woman (Tamara Garina),
He-Wolf (Michael Baseleon), Leaping Buck (Manuel Padilla),
the medicine man for Sun Vow ritual (Iron Eyes Cody),
and Striking Bear (Terry Leonard). A critic in Film
Quarterly comments, "Stripped of its pretentions, Horse
parades the standard myth that the white man can do

everything better than the Indian. Give him a little
time and he will marry the best-looking girl (a princess
of course) and will end up chief of the tribe." (Spring
1972, 28)

740 The McMasters (Chevron 1970) Alf Kjellin
     After the black hero helps White Feather (David Car-
     radine), the Indian gives him his sister, Robin (Nancy
     Kwan) whom the hero first rapes and then marries. At
     the end the Indians rescue the hero who finally decides
     to live on the ranch with Robin rather than with them.
     A Variety critic notes that the film "skillfully deals with
     tensions and prejudices that lead to violence and leave
     no one the winner." (17 June)

741 The Red, White and Black (Hirschman-Northern 1970)
     John Cardos
     When a brave is killed, the Indians, two of whom are
     Chief Walking Horse (Robert Dix) and Kayitah (Bobby
     Clark) attack some black soldiers.

742 Run Simon Run (Aaron Spelling 1970) George McGowan
     A Papago Indian released from prison, Simon Zuniga
     (Burt Reynolds) searches for the killer of his brother.
     Other Indian characters are Manuel (Rudolfo Acosta),
     Asa (Herman Rudin), and Santana (Eddie Little Sky).

743 Soldier Blue (Avco-Embassy) Ralph Nelson
     In this film based on Theodore Olson's novel Arrow
     in the Sun, some Cheyenne, two of whom are Spotted
     Wolf (Jorge Rivero) and Running Fox (Jorge Russek),
     slaughter a party of soldiers. A cavalry unit bent on
     revenge attacks the tribe at Sand Creek despite the ef-
     forts of a white woman to save them. A Variety critic
     comments, "The climax of the film ... makes the Army
     the complete villain and the Cheyennes complete inno-
     cents. The seemingly handful of warriors are quickly
     wiped out, the women raped, children mutilated and, in
     many cases, murdered." (12 Aug)

744 Song of the Loon (Hollywood Cinema Assoc. 1970) Andrew
     Herbert
     Singing Heron (John Kalfas), Acomas (Martin Valez),
     Tsi-Nokha (Brad Dela Vale), Tiasholah (Michael Traxon),
     Bear-Who-Dreams (Lucky Manning), and other members
     of the tribe teach a homosexual man about sexual love.

1971

745   The Animals (Levitt-Pickman 1971) Ron Joy
        Chatto (Henry Silva) rescues a white woman who has
      been raped and helps her track down and kill the rapists.
      He is then killed by a posse and at the end of the film
      the Apaches are ready to get their revenge by attacking
      the posse.

746   Billy Jack (Warner 1971) T.C. Frank (Tom Laughlin)
        Billy Jack, a half-breed Vietnam veteran, defends In-
      dian children and the white woman who teaches them at
      the reservation school from villains in the nearby town.
      A Variety critic notes that "the plight of the American
      Indian, the prejudices against and the refusal of many
      to accept him are pinpointed." (5 May) An NYT critic
      comments, "There is something of Sgt. York about Billy
      Jack, who is described as a war-hero (an ex-Green
      Beret) who hates war, and something of both Tonto and
      the Lone Ranger.... He is a comic strip character with
      delusions of philosophic grandeur." (11 Mar 1973, 1)

747   Captain Apache (Scotia Inter. 1971) Alexander Singer
        Captain Apache (Lee Van Cleef) is an Indian Union
      officer who investigates the murder of an Indian agent.

748   Deserter (Paramount 1971) Burt Kennedy
        An Indian-hating hero leads a unit of Indian fighters
      against the Apache, two of whom are Natchai (Ricardo
      Montalban) and Chief Durango (Mimmo Palmara). An NYT
      critic notes that "the deserter is an Army captain, shat-
      tered by the Apache's horrible mutilation of his wife (an
      opening that will chill you), who takes to the old South-
      west hills as a one-man Indian butcher." (10 June 49)

749   Man in the Wilderness (Warner 1971) Richard Sarafian
        An Indian chief (Henry Wilcoxon) helps the hero get
      his revenge on the villains.

1972

750   The Bravos (Universal 1972) Ted Post
        Indians led by Santana (Joaquin Martinez) kidnap the
      hero's son.

751   Buck and the Preacher (Columbia 1972) Sidney Poitier
        The two black heroes deal with Sinsie (Julie Robinson)
      who speaks for her brother the Chief (Enrique Lucero).
      An NYT critic comments, "The movie West, of course, has
      never been completely lilly-white. There have always
      been a certain number of Indians horsing around, scalp-
      ing, drinking, shooting, getting shot, and being poorly
      dealt with by just about everybody, including the movie-
      makers." (29 Apr 19)

752   Cancel My Reservation (Warner 1972) Paul Bogart
        The hero (Bob Hope) tries to solve the murder of
      Mary Little Cloud (Betty Carr) with the help of Crazy
      (Anne Archer), Joe Little Cloud (Henry Darrow) and
      Old Bear (Chief Dan George), an Indian mystic.

753   Chato's Land (UA 1972) Michael Winner
        A posse pursues Chato (Charles Bronson), an Apache
      leader. A Variety critic comments that the "narrative
      is fleshed out when the Indian reverts to a savage venge-
      ful warrior after a few members of posse rape his squaw
      and the roles of hunter and hunted are reversed." (17
      May)

754   Climb an Angry Mountain (Warner 1972) Leonard Horn
        Lawmen pursue an Indian, Joey Chilko (Joe Kapp) up
      the side of Mount Shasta.

755   House Made of Dawn (Firebird 1972) Richardson Morse
        In this film based on N. Scott Momaday's novel, Abel
      (Larry Littlebird) a veteran, is torn between living on
      the reservation of his grandfather (Mesa Bird) or in the
      city with his friend Ben Benally (Jay Varela) and the In-
      dian minister, Tosamah (John Saxon). (See pages 140-
      43 for further discussion of this film.)

756   Jeremiah Johnson (Warner 1972) S. Pollack
        Johnson (Robert Redford) violates a Crow burial
      ground by riding through it, and the Indians, who had
      been his friends, kill his Indian wife (Delle Bolton) and
      adopted son. He then takes revenge by killing many of
      them until the Crow's chief, Painted Shirt (Joaquin Mar-
      tinez), makes peace as a sign of respect for his bravery.
      A Variety critic notes that the film provides a "newer
      look at Indian-white man relations, without branding either

as good or bad but of differing, yet clearcut, cultures
that could have existed side by side with some understanding." (10 May)

757 Journey Through Rosebud (GSF 1972) Tom Gries
     The hero, a draft dodger who drifts onto the Rosebud
Sioux Reservation, makes friends with Frank (Robert
Forster), an alcoholic and rebellious Sioux Vietnam veter-
an. He learns about Indian customs and problems, and
falls in love with Shirley (Victoria Racimo), the activist
ex-wife of Frank. At the end Frank commits suicide.
Other Indian characters are John (Steven Shemayne),
Stanley Pike (Eddie Little Sky) and Mrs. Blackwing (Diane Running). A Newsweek critic notes that "these
sentimentalized Indians seem no more real, arouse little
more compassion than the ones who used to bite the dust
every Saturday in B Westerns." (24 April 89)

758 The Loners (Fanfare 1972) Sutton Roley
     The hero, a half-breed Navajo who wants to be a
motorcycle racer, gets in trouble and ends up in a shoot-
out at his father's (Hal Jon Norman) hogan.

759 The New Land (Svensk Film 1972) Jan Troell
     This Swedish film about the trials of Scandinavian im-
migrants to the Midwest depicts the uprising of Sioux
who had been mistreated by the government and the sub-
sequent hanging of almost 40 of them.

760 Ulzana's Raid (Universal 1972) Robert Aldrich
     The hero, an old Indian fighter, and his men, one of
whom is an Apache scout, Ke-Ni-Tays (Jorge Luke),
hunt down Ulzana (Joaquin Martinez) and nine Apache
braves who have fled the reservation.

761 When the Legends Die (20th Cent-Fox 1972) Stuart Millar
     In this film based on Hal Borland's novel, Tom Black
Bull (Robert Forster), a Ute, is taken from the wilderness and his pet bear to a reservation school by Blue
Elk (John War Eagle). After becoming a champion bronc
rider with the help of a hard-drinking white man who is
both a father figure and an oppressor, Tom, frustrated
with rodeos and white women, decides to return to his
reservation. A Time critic comments: "When the Legends
Die is one of the rare movies that seem genuinely to ex-

press, even in a small way, the strangled rage and un-
certainty of the modern Indian." (6 Nov 86)

1973

762 Alien Thunder (Canadian 1973) Claude Fournier
     In this film with Chief Dan George, a Mountie pur-
sues a Cree accused of murder.

763 Billy Two Hats (UA 1973) Ted Kotcheff
     Billy (Desi Arnaz, Jr.), a half-breed Kiowa who is
on the run, falls in love with a mail-order-bride and,
along with the hero, fights Apaches.

764 Blazing Saddles (Warner 1973) Mel Brooks
     In this burlesque of westerns, the Indian Chief (Mel
Brooks) speaks Yiddish.

765 Cahill, U.S. Marshall (Warner 1973) Andrew V. McLaglen
     Lightfoot (Neville Brand), a half-breed Comanche
tracker, is the wise and loyal friend of the hero.

766 Charley One Eye (Paramount 1973) Don Chaffey
     A black man and a stoic crippled Indian join together
and have a strange kind of friendship because they are
both outcasts. A critic from New York Magazine comments: "Its intention, I suspect, was to prove the noble
simplicity of the red man, but it manages to state that by
sheer stupidity that borders on mental retardation the
Indian is less maniacally vicious than the black, Mexican
or white man." (23 April 72)

767 Chino (Italian 1973) John Sturges
     Chino (Charles Bronson), a half-breed, fights the
villains to keep control of his horse ranch.

768 Cotter (Independent 1973) Paul Stanley
     Cotter (Don Murray), a Sioux rodeo clown with a
drinking problem, returns to his homeland only to be
wrongly blamed for the murder of a rancher because he
is a drunken Indian.

769 I Heard the Owl Call My Name (Tomorrow Enter. 1973)
Daryl Duke

In this film based on Margaret Craven's novel, a dying priest learns about life from the Indians, two of whom are Keetah (Marianne Jones) and George Hudson (George Clutesi).

770 Injun Fender (Duke U. 1973) Robert Cordier
In this student film, an Indian rock musician named Fender (Dennis Campbell) kills several whites.

771 One Little Indian (Buena Vista 1973) Bernard McEveety
The hero, in trouble for trying to save the lives of Indian women and children during a cavalry raid, befriends a boy raised by the Indians who eventually helps the hero prove his innocence. One of the Indians is Jimmy Wolf (Jay Silverheels).

772 Santee (Crown Inter. 1973) Gary Nelson
John Crow (Jay Silverheels) is the loyal friend of the hero.

773 Tom Sawyer (UA 1973) Don Taylor
Injun Joe (Kunu Hank) is the villain in this musical version of Twain's novel. A Variety critic notes that "Hank is vividly menacing." (14 Mar)

1974

774 Harry and Tonto (20th Cent-Fox 1974) Paul Mazursky
The hero meets a humorous old Indian (Chief Dan George) in jail.

775 Nakia (Screen Gems 1974) Leonard Horn
A Navajo deputy sheriff, Nakia Parker (Robert Forster), gets in trouble when the Indians of his tribe, two of whom are Naiche (George Clutesi) and Diane Little Eagle (Maria Eleva Cordero), try to save a mission from white developers.

776 Trial of Billy Jack (Taylor-Laughlin 1974) Tom Laughlin
In this sequel to the popular Billy Jack (1971), the half-breed hero returns from prison to deal with whites who are mistreating Indians from the reservation school. Other Indian characters are Blue Elk (Guy Greymountain), Patsy Littlejohn (Sacheen Littlefeather), Thunder Mountain

(Rolling Thunder), Little Bear (Buffalo Horse), Sunshine
(Susan Sosa), and Oshannah (Oshannah Fastwolf).

777   The White Dawn (Paramount 1974) Philip Kaufman
      In this film based on James Huston's An Eskimo Saga,
the behavior of three whalers stranded among the Eskimos,
one of whom is in love with an Eskimo woman, Neevee
(Pilitak), leads to serious trouble. Other Eskimo characters are the Shaman (Sagiaktok), Sowniapik (Munamee
Sake), and his wife (Pitseolala Kili). A Variety critic
notes that "supporting players, all Eskimos, are excel-
lent to the last character ... they speak their own language, with subtitles, a sensible touch." (17 July)

                              1975

778   Against a Crooked Sky (Doty-Dayton 1975) Earl Bellamy
      After the Indians of Temkai (Geoffrey Land) kidnap
a young woman, the heroes struggle with them to rescue her. Other Indian characters are Shumeki (Gordon
Hanson) and Cut Tongue (Henry Wilcoxon). A Variety
critic comments, "Against a Crooked Sky is an oater which
harks back to the not-so-good old days when Indians
were depicted as lascivious villains bent on kidnapping
white girls and murdering pet dogs.... It's amazing
that this film was made in 1975." (24 Dec)

779   I Will Fight No More Forever (Wolper 1975) Richard Hef-
fron
      The Nez Percé Indians of Chief Joseph (Ned Romero),
who don't want to be put on a reservation, fight the
U.S. cavalry as they attempt to escape into Canada.
Other Indian characters are Wahletis (John Kauffman),
Olloket (Emilio Delgato), Rainbow (Nick Ramus), Toma
(Linda Redfearn), White Bird (Frank Salsedo), and
Looking Glass (Vincent St. Cyr).

780   One Flew Over the Cuckoo's Nest (UA 1975) Milos For-
man
      In this film based on Ken Kesey's novel, Chief Brom-
den (Will Sampson) is the hero's friend. A New Yorker
critic comments: "The film has its climactic Indian-white
love-death, and at the end Kesey's reversal of the American legend (now the white man is sacrificed for the In-

dian) is satisfying on the deepest pop-myth level." (1
Dec. 134)

781 Rancho Deluxe (UA 1975) Frank Perry
     The hero lives it up with Cecil Colson (Sam Waterston),
"a literate and spaced-out Indian" who "makes jokes about
being an Indian" (NYT 24 Nov 75), and they both end
up in prison.

782 Rooster Cogburn (Universal 1975) Stuart Millar
     Villains kill a minister and some of his Indian wards.
Wolf (Richard Romancito), who is a young Indian, and
the minister's daughter, work together with the hero to
bring the villains to justice.

                              1976

783 Breakheart Pass (UA 1976) Tom Gries
     Paiutes, one of whom is White Hand (Eddie Little Sky),
conspire with the villains and threaten people on a train.

784 Bridger (Universal 1976) David Lowell Rich
     The hero deals with Indians, among whom are a Sho-
shone Woman (Margarita Cordova), a Crow chief (X.
Brands), a Paiute chief (Skeeter Vaughn) and a Modoc
leader (Robert Miano), as he blazes a trail across the
Rockies to California.

785 Buffalo Bill and the Indians or Sitting Bull's History
     Lesson (UA 1976) Robert Altman
     In this film based on Arthur Kopit's play Indians,
Buffalo Bill Cody (Paul Newman), a strange character
with quirks--like a hatred of song birds and a passion
for operatic sopranos--deals with Sitting Bull (Frank
Kaquitts) and his Indian interpreter, William Halsey (Will
Sampson), as performers in his Wild West Show. At the
end Cody shows his craziness as he symbolically triumphs
over Sitting Bull in a fake battle in the show.

786 The Great Scout and Cathouse Thursday (American Inter.
     1976) Don Taylor
     In this comedy, Joe Knox is an educated Indian friend
of the hero who joins him to get revenge on a partner
who cheated them. A Variety critic comments on this

character who thinks he can get back at the whites by infecting them with syphilis: "Reed's role is a hammy embarrassment." (16 June)

787 Joe Panther (Artists' Creation 1976) Paul Krasny
     This film based on the novel by Zachary Bell tells the story of Joe Panther (Ray Tracey), a Seminole who fights alligators; his friend Billy Tiger (A. Martinez); and Turtle George (Ricardo Montalban), an Indian wise man who gives the young men advice. Other Indian characters are Tommy Panther (Gem Thorpe Osceola), Joe's mother (Lois Red Elk), and Jenny Rainbow (Monika Ramirey). A Variety critic comments, "Where the film fudges is in its simplistic treatment of the Indian's struggles with white society.... The problem is much more complex than the film's rosy resolution makes it seem...." (3 Nov)

788 Mustang County (Universal 1976) John Champion
     Nika (Nika Mina) is the young Indian companion of the hero who treats him with "pleasant fatherly wisdom and kindness." (Var 24 Mar)

789 The Outlaw Josey Wales (Warner 1976) Clint Eastwood
     During his quest for revenge, the hero meets Lone Watie (Chief Dan George), a wise old Indian with a sense of humor, Chato (John Verros), Ten Bears (Will Sampson), and Little Moonlight (Geraldine Keams). A New York critic notes that she is "the first convincing movie Indian girl, and, indeed, Miss Keams is a genuine Navajo." (6 Sept 76)

790 The Return of a Man Called Horse (UA 1976) Irvin Kershner
     In this sequel, John Morgan (Richard Harris) returns to his adopted Yellow Hand tribe. After more Sun Vow torture and visions during sweats and fasts, he helps them triumph over villainous trappers who have taken their land. The Indian characters are Elk Woman (Gale Sondergaard), Running Bull (Jorge Luke), Raven (Enrique Lucero), Moonstar (Ana De Sade), Standing Bear (Pedro Damlen), Thin Dog (Humberto Lopey-Pineda), Grey Thorn (Patricia Reyes), Lame Wolf (Regino Herrerra), Owl (Rigoberto Rico), and Red Cloud (Alberto Marsical). A Time critic comments, "The movie is too

glib about Indian spirituality to be good, too selfconscious
about being on the Indians' side to be wholly convincing."
(13 Sept 80) A New Yorker critic remarks, "The attitude of the film toward Indians is patronizing in the extreme. It feeds notions about the Western white man as
omniscient savior which are already too current." (16
Aug 87)

791 Shadow of the Hawk (Columbia 1976) George McCowan
     Old Man Hawk (Chief Dan George), a medicine man,
brings his grandson (Jan-Michael Vincent) from the city
and teaches him the arts of magic so he can fight the
evil spirits loosed by the evil tribal witch, Dsonoqua
(Marianne Jones).

792 Winterhawk (Howco Inter. 1976) Charles B. Pierce
     Winterhawk (Michael Dante), a Blackfoot chief, is
attacked while he is traveling in peace to get serum for
the smallpox which is killing his people. He gets his
revenge by kidnapping two white children. Other Indian characters are Red Calf (Ace Powell) and Pale Flower (Sacheen Littlefeather). A Variety critic comments
that "like Ford in Cheyenne Autumn (though on a far
less grandiose level of failure), Pierce can't get inside
the Indians he is trying to ennoble. Title character
Michael Dante is little more than a cigar store Indian,
speaking pidgin English and gazing balefully at the horizon." (28 Jan)

1977

793 Billy Jack Goes to Washington (Taylor-Laughlin 1977)
Tom Laughlin
     In this second sequel to Billy Jack (1971), the half-
breed hero (Tom Laughlin) deals with the U.S. Government.

794 Grayeagle (Howco Inter. 1977) Charles B. Pierce
     After Grayeagle (Alex Cord), a Cheyenne, abducts a
white girl who is really the daughter of the Cheyenne
chief, the trapper she lived with and his Indian friend
(Iron Eyes Cody) pursue Grayeagle and battle with Sho-
shones.

795 Guardian of the Wilderness (Sunn Classics 1977) David
O'Malley
     Teneiya (Don Shanks) is an Indian friend of the hero

who helps him build a cabin in the wilderness.

796 The Incredible Rocky Mountain Race (Schick Sunn 1977)
     James L. Conway
       Eagle Feather (Larry Storch), a somewhat crazy In-
     dian, helps the hero in the race. Crazy Horse (Mike
     Mazurki) is another Indian character in this TV movie.

797 Last of the Mohicans (Schick Sunn 1977) James L. Conway
       This TV movie retells Cooper's story of Hawkeye (Steve
     Forrest), Chingachgook (Ned Romero), Uncas (Don Shanks),
     and Magua (Robert Tessier).

798 Orca (Paramount 1977) Michael Anderson
       Umilak (Will Sampson), an Indian whom an NYT critic
     describes as a "font of Indian lore," is finally killed by
     Orca, a killer whale.

799 Three Warriors (Fantasy Films 1977) Keith Merrill
       Michael (McKee Redwing), a young urban Indian who
     is ashamed of his heritage, has to visit his ailing grand-
     father (Charles White Eagle) on the reservation. At a
     camp in the woods the old man teaches him Indian lore,
     and tells him of the goodness of his father who died in
     an accident caused by drinking. After he learns to ride
     a horse his grandfather bought him, Michael shows his
     bravery and calls the horse Three Warriors--for the old
     man, his father and himself. At the end, when Michael
     leaves for the city, he has a strong new appreciation of
     what it means to be Indian.

800 The White Buffalo (UA 1977) J. Lee Thompson
       As Crazy Horse (Will Sampson) and Wild Bill Hickok
     (Charles Bronson) struggle to be the first to kill the mythical
     white buffalo, a kind of respect grows between the two men.

1978

801 Centennial (Universal 1978-9) Virgil Vogel
       In this TV mini-series based on James Michener's
     novel, Indian characters--Tame Beaver (Michael Ansara),
     Clay Backet (Barbara Carrera), Old Sioux (Chief Dan
     George), Blue Leaf (Maria Potts), Broken Thumb (Jorge
     Rivero), and Lost Eagle (Nick Ramus)--appear in chap-
     ters entitled "For as Long as the Water Flows" and "The
     Massacre."

802   The Deerslayer (Schick Sunn 1978) Dick Friedenberg
          In this TV movie based on Cooper's novel, Hawkeye
       (Steve Forrest) and Chingachgook (Ned Romero) deal
       with the Hurons of Chief Rivenoak (Victor Mohica).

803   Ishi: The Last of His Tribe (E.M. Lewis 1978) Robert
       E. Miller
          Based on the book Ishi in Two Worlds by Theodora
       Kroeber Quinn, this film tells the story of Ishi (Elroy
       Phil Casados), the last survivor of the Yahi tribe, from
       his childhood through his friendship with an anthropolo-
       gist to his death in 1917.   Other Indian characters are
       played by Lois Red Elk and Joseph Running Fox.

804   The Manitou (Avco Embassy) William Girdler
          Standing Rock (Michael Ansara), a contemporary Sioux
       medicine man, struggles to exorcise a four-hundred-year-
       old demon spirit of a medicine man which has attached it-
       self to the back of a white woman.

805   Marie-Anne (Canadian 1978) R. Martin Walters
          A white woman, Louis Riel's grandmother, must deal
       with an offer of marriage from Chief Many Horses (Gordon
       Tootoosie) and the irate Indian commonlaw wife (Tantoo
       Martin) of her husband.   A Variety critic notes, "There's
       a nice twist in having the girl adopted by an Indian tribe
       in order to calm both sides...."   (2 Aug)

                              1979

806   Dreamspeaker (CBC 1979) Claude Jutra
          In this Canadian film, an emotionally disturbed white
       boy is taken in by an Indian shaman (George Clutesi),
       along with a mute.   Although the old Indian brings some
       joy and healing to the boy and the mute through his
       knowledge of the old ways, they cannot handle white so-
       ciety and after the old man dies both commit suicide.

807   Eagle's Wing (Rank 1979) Anthony Harvey
          During his struggles with a white man for the pos-
       session of the horse Eagle's Wing, White Bull (Sam Water-
       ston) attacks a stage and carries off a white woman.

808   Mr. Horn (Lorimar 1979) Jack Starrett

One of the exploits of the hero is hunting down and
capturing Geronimo (Enrique Lucero).

809 Nightwing (Columbia 1979) Arthur Hiller
     Youngman Duran (Nick Mancuso), a tribal policeman
who loves a white woman, and Walker Chee (Stephen
Macht) deal with vampire bats loosed by tribal magic in
a film referred to as a "mixture of Indian occultism, native rights, pseudo-science and romance." (Variety 4
July) Another Indian character is Abner Tasupi (George
Clutesi).

810 Old Fish Hawk (CFDC 1979) Donald Shebib
     After smallpox kills his family, Fish Hawk (Will Samp-
son) lives among the whites and survives by drinking until he meets a young white boy. At the end the boy rejects him when Fish Hawk refuses to kill an old wild boar
because the animal reminds him of himself.

811 The Villain (Columbia 1979) Hal Needham
     Nervous Elk (Paul Lynde) is an effeminate Indian chief
in this spoof of westerns which makes fun of the Indian
rites of the pipe and drum, their horsemanship, treatment of white women and rights to their own land.

                            1980

812 Altered States (Warner 1980) Ken Russell
     In Mexico the hero engages in a mystical Indian rite
conducted by the Brujo (Charles White Eagle).

813 Bronco Billy (Warner 1980) Clint Eastwood
     Chief Big Eagle (Dan Vadis) and his wife, Lorraine
Running Water (Sierra Pecheur), are down-on-their-luck
Indian snake dancers who join Bronco Billy's traveling
show.

814 The Mountain Men (Columbia 1980) Richard Lang
     The hero and Heavy Eagle (Stephen Macht) fight over
the possession of Running Moon (Victoria Racimo) in a
film with bloody hand-to-hand battles. Other Indian
characters are Medicine Wolf (David Ackroyd), Cross
Otter (Cal Bellini), Iron Belly (Victor Jory), and the
Blackfoot chief (Danny Zapien). An NYT critic comments,

"In the true spirit of tokenism, these Indians are given
a few extra speeches about how badly 'the long knives'
have treated them. But because the Indian leader Heavy
Eagle is played with particular hamminess by Stephen
Macht, the Indians seem sadly ill-treated here anyhow."
(13 Sept 1)

815 Windwalker (Pacific Inter. 1980) Keith Merrill
        In this film based on the Blaine Yorgason novel,
     Windwalker, a Cheyenne, is seen as an old man (Trevor
     Howard) and as a young man (James Remar) who loses
     his wife, Tashina (Serene Hedin), and his two sons to
     the Crow, his traditional enemies. After years of search-
     ing, the old Windwalker protects what is left of his family
     from the Crow, one of whom is his missing son (Nick
     Ramus). At the end he is reunited with his son and then
     goes to the spirit world to be with Tashina.
        Other Indian characters are Dancing Moon (Dusty Iron
     Wing McCrea), Little Feather (Silvana Gallardo), Crow
     Scout (Billy Drago), Crow Eyes (Rudy Diaz), Crow Hair
     (Harold Goss-Coyote), Wounded Crow (Roy J. Cohoe),
     Horse That Follows (Jason Stevens), and Happy Wind
     (Roberta Deherrera). A Variety critic, noting the use
     of Indian language on the sound track, comments,
     "Coupled with the absence of non-Indian characters in
     the film, which takes place in the 18th century, this gives
     the Indians on screen a dignity they have been denied
     previously, even in the most sympathetic of westerns."
     (10 Dec).

                            1981

816 The Legend of the Lone Ranger (Universal 1981) William
     A. Fraker
        The hero and Tonto (Michael Horse) rescue President
     Grant in a film in which "Indians are presented in a
     more modernist, revisionist light, while Grant and his
     group (Hickok, Custer, Cody) are presented as near
     comedians." (Var 20 May) At the end of the film, when
     Grant asks how he can show his gratitude, Tonto tells
     him to honor the treaties with the Indians.

817 The Wolfen (Orion 1981) Michael Wadleigh
        In this thriller the Wolfen are wolf-like spirits of In-

dians who prey on New Yorkers. The Indian characters
are a politically active steelworker (Edward J. Olmos)
and an old man (Dehl Berti). A Newsweek critic comments, "Though the movie pretends it's championing the
Indians, it defames them, and though it implies it's striking a blow for the disinherited, it also suggests that the
South Bronx is better off in ruins." (3 Aug 51)

1982

818 The Legend of Walks Far Woman (NBC 1982) Mel Adamski
     This TV film tells the story of an Indian woman (Ra-
quel Welch) from youth to old age at the time of the battle of Little Big Horn. An NYT critic comments, "It's
just that the entire story is boring as it trudges through
clichés about Indian nobility and the stupid ways of
white man, who does not even know enough to live in
portable houses." (28 May 26)

819 Sacred Ground (Independent 1982) Charles B. Pierce
     A white man and his family build their cabin on ground
sacred to the Indians. They are attacked and then the
man seeks revenge.

820 Spirit of the Wind (Doyon Ltd. 1982) Ralph Liddle
     This film tells the story of George Attla, Jr. (Pius
Savage), the famous Alaskan Indian dogsled racer. Oth-
er Indian characters are George Attla, Sr. (George
Clutesi), Moses (Chief Dan George), and George Attla
Jr.'s mother (Rose Attla Ambrose). (See pages 140-43
for further discussion of this film.)

1983

821 48 Hours (Paramount 1983) Walter Hill
     Billy Bear (Sonny Landham) is the violent Indian
friend of the psychopathic villain.

822 Running Brave (Buena Vista 1983) D.S. Everett (Donald
     Shebib)
     This film tells the story of Billy Mills (Robby Benson)
a Sioux Indian who became an Olympic champion in long-
distance running. Billy deals with prejudice at the Uni-

versity of Kansas, the strain of a mixed marriage and his
troubled relationship with his family on the Sioux reservation, two of whom are his father (August Schellenberg)
and his brother Frank (Denis Lacrois), an alcoholic
artist who finally commits suicide. A Variety critic notes
that "Billy's Indian relatives come and go throughout the
picture as stereotypical Indians. One is bitter and hate-
ful of white men, the other is a crushed alcoholic with
unrealized talent." (5 Oct)

823 Second Thoughts (Independent 1983) Laurence Turman
        The hero, a half-breed whose Indian name is William
     Littlehorse (Craig Wesson), falls in love with a white
     female lawyer.

824 Triumph of a Man Called Horse (Classic 1983) John Hough
        In this sequel to A Man Called Horse (1970), Horse's
     son Koda (Michael Beck), a half-breed Sioux, and Koda's
     lover, Redwing (Ana de Sade) a Crow Woman, foil the
     attempts of villains trying to start a war with the Sioux
     so they can get the gold in the Black Hills.

                              1984

825 Firestarter (Universal 1984) Mark Lester
        John Rainbird (George C. Scott) is a sinister Indian
     villain who works for the government.

826 Fleshburn (Crown Inter. 1984) George Gage
        Calvin Duggai (Sonny Landham), a Navajo, escapes
     from a mental institution and takes revenge on those
     who testified against him by stranding them in a desert.

827 Harold of Orange (Film in the Cities 1984) Richard Weise
        In this short film, modern tricksters Harold Sinseer
     (Charlie Hill), Son Bear (Bruce Murray), and New Crows
     (Deforest White Eagle) con a board of directors into a
     grant for growing pinchbeans on the reservation.

828 The Mystic Warrior (Wolper 1984) Richard Heffron
        In this TV mini-series based on Ruth Beebe Hill's
     Hanta Yo, a young Sioux warrior, Ahbleza (Robert Bel-
     tran), falls in love with a beautiful Indian woman (Devon
     Erickson) and becomes the leader and savior of his tribe.

Indians and scholars fought this project from the
beginning and a Newsweek critic quotes the reaction of
an Indian anthropologist to the revised script: "'It's
still a bunch of Hollywood pap,' Archambault told a re-
porter. 'They're still having us speak Hiawatha English,
as if we really walked around saying "Many horses have
I."'" (21 May 76)

829 Never Cry Wolf (Buena Vista 1984) Carroll Ballard
      The hero learns about wolves from the Inuit wise
      man Ootek (Zachary Iitimangnag), who tells him the myth
      of the wolf spirit, and deals with Mike (Samson Jorah),
      the Inuit hunter who kills wolves to make money.

830 Return of the Country (Independent 1984) Bob Hicks
     (a Creek-Seminole)
      A white woman who is the newly appointed BIA Com-
      missioner is transported to a world where an Indian
      Bureau of White Affairs watches over whites.

CONCLUSION: BEYOND THE FICTIONAL INDIAN

The following disclaimer at the end of modern films is an important reminder that film is a form of fictional literature: "All Characters and Incidents in this Film Are Fictitious. Any Correspondence Between Real People, either Living or Dead, Is Purely Coincidental." Certainly any correspondence between the Indians in narrative film and real American Indians is purely coincidental. Critics who deplore the lack of historical accuracy in the portrayal of Indians sometimes expect more from film than it will ever have to offer. Film historian Jon Tuska acknowledges this, when after considering the mixed messages about Indians in westerns, he writes: "It has been my experience that ... one does not go to movies--and Westerns most of all--to obtain a balanced view or accurate history" (538). Even Indian actors are resigned to the fiction, as a spokesman indicates: "Indian actors understand about the Indian's portrayal on the screen, but, like any other race, we would prefer having historic truths shown, and would like to see ourselves depicted in a kindlier manner than in most wild and woolly westerns" (Spears 396). There is, of course, no question that "the wild and woolly westerns" have fixed negative images of Indians in the minds of their audiences, but at least the first step to better understanding is an awareness of the fiction.

When film audiences realize that they are getting not history but fiction in westerns, they will begin to know that they must not be believed; rather they must be interpreted. As the summaries of the plots have suggested, once this process starts the central theme of the westerns, i.e., the superiority of the male heroes, is rather easy to see. This provides a basis for understanding why the films portray Indians, or, for that matter, other minorities and women, as always either too good or bad. On this narrative level the central theme can be seen for what it is and, in a sense, interpreted away. The same is not true for the visual images of Indians expressed by the medium of film.

Dealing with the images is more complicated because they have become ingrained in our memories. For example, my dominant image is that of looking up into the kindly eyes of Old Lodge Skins as he sits in his tepee; whereas, a friend sees an image of the silhouette of Geronimo disguised as a soldier walking stiffly up to kill a sentry, after which his face appears in a terrifying close-up. Film goers are biased by so many images like these (and the messages about Indians they suggest) that they feel they "know" Indians, even though many really know little or nothing about Native American history or culture. Such influence can't be explained away like the themes, but even a rudimentary knowledge of the film language used to express and give impact to the images will help audiences to understand a little better the process of encoding that establishes the fictional Indian.

In 1967 an Indian leader considered the effect of the fictional Indian on his children: "I think they wonder, when are we going to win? I remember seeing such a movie when one of my boys was a kid. We came out of the movies, and he pulled my hand and said, 'Daddy, we pretty near won that one' " (Armstrong 155).

If audiences can get beyond the fictional Indian through an awareness of how film works as a fictional literature and how it communicates through basic film techniques such as camera angles, composition, editing, music and acting, maybe the real Indians will finally win one.

WORKS CITED

Armstrong, Virginia I., ed. I Have Spoken, American History Through the Voices of Indians. Athens, OH: The Swallow Press, 1971.

Biskind, Peter. Seeing Is Believing: How Hollywood Taught Us to Stop Worrying and Love the Fifties. New York: Pantheon Books, 1983.

Bogdanovich, Peter. John Ford. Berkeley: University of California Press, 1968.

Bowser, Eileen, comp. Biograph Bulletins 1908-1912. New York: Farrar, Straus and Giroux, 1973.

Brownlow, Kevin. The War, the West and the Wilderness. New York: Alfred A. Knopf, 1979.

Calder, Jenni. There Must Be a Lone Ranger: The American West in Film and in Reality. New York: McGraw-Hill, 1977.

Friar, Ralph E. and Natasha A. The Only Good Indian ...: The Hollywood Gospel. New York: Drama Book Specialists, 1972.

Marsden, Michael, and Jack Nachbar. "Images of Native Americans in Popular Film," Course File, AFI Education Newsletter, Sept-Oct, 1980, 4-7.

Niver, Kemp R., comp. Biograph Bulletins 1896-1908. Los Angeles: Artisan Press, 1971.

O'Connor, John E. The Hollywood Indian: Stereotypes of Native Americans in Films. Trenton, NJ: New Jersey State Museum, 1980.

Parish, James R., and Michael R. Pitts. The Great Western Pictures. Metuchen, NJ: Scarecrow Press, 1976.

Price, John A. "The Stereotyping of North American Indians in Motion Pictures," The Pretend Indian. Eds. Gretchen M. Bataille and Charles L. Silet. Ames: Iowa State University Press, 1980.

Spears, Jack. "The Indian on the Screen," Hollywood: The Golden Era. New York: A.S. Barnes, 1971.

Spehr, Paul C. The Movies Begin: Making Movies in New Jersey
   1887-1920. Newark, NJ: Newark Museum, 1977.

Stedman, Raymond W. Shadows of the Indian. Norman: University
   of Oklahoma Press, 1982.

Tuska, Jon. The Filming of the West. New York: Doubleday & Co.,
   1976.

Variety Film Reviews: 1907-1980. 16 Vols. New York: Garland
   Press, 1983.

Weaver, John T. Twenty Years of Silents. Metuchen, NJ: Scarecrow Press, 1971.

SELECTIVE BIBLIOGRAPHY

Adams, Les, and Buck Rainey. Shoot-Em-Ups: A Complete Reference Guide to Westerns of the Sound Era. New Rochelle, NY:
Arlington House, 1978; reprint, Metuchen, NJ: Scarecrow Press,
1986.

Alvarez, Max J. Index to Motion Pictures Reviewed by Variety 1907-
1980. Metuchen, NJ: Scarecrow Press, 1982.

Balshofer, Fred J., and Arthur C. Miller. One Reel a Week. Berkeley: University of California Press, 1967.

Bataille, Gretchen M., and Charles L.P. Silet, eds. "Annotated
Checklist of Articles and Books on the Popular Images of the In-
dian in the American Film," The Pretend Indian. Ames: Iowa
State University Press, 1980.

Frayling, Christopher. Spaghetti Westerns. London: Routledge,
Kegan Paul, 1981.

French, Philip. Westerns: Aspects of a Movie Genre. London:
Secker and Warburg, 1973.

Garfield, Brian. Western Films. New York: Rawson Assoc., 1982.

Henderson, Robert M. D.W. Griffith: The Years at Biograph. New
York: Farrar, Straus and Giroux, 1970.

Krafsur, Richard P., ed. The American Film Institute Catalogue:
Feature Films 1961-1970. New York: R.R. Bowker, 1976.

Leonard, Harold, ed. The Film Index: A Bibliography. Vol. 1
The Film as Art. New York: Museum of Modern Art Film Library
and the H.W. Wilson Co., 1941.

Miller, Randall M., ed. The Kaleidoscopic Lens: How Hollywood
Views the Ethnic Groups. Jerome S. Ozer, Publisher, 1980.

Munden, Kenneth W. The American Film Institute Catalogue: Feature
Films 1921-1930. New York: R.R. Bowker, 1971.

Nachbar, John G., ed. Focus on the Western. Englewood Cliffs, NJ:
Prentice-Hall, 1974.

_____. Western Films: An Annotated Critical Bibliography. New
    York: Garland, 1975.

New York Times Film Reviews: 1913-1980. 12 Vols. New York:
    New York Times and Arno Press, 1981.

O'Connor, John E., and Martin A. Jackson, eds. American History/
    American Film: Interpreting the Hollywood Image. New York:
    Ungar, 1979.

Pilkington, William T., and Don Graham. Western Movies. Albuquer-
    que: University of New Mexico Press, 1979.

Place, J.A. The Western Films of John Ford. New York: Citadel,
    1974.

Rothel, David. Who Was That Masked Man? The Story of the Lone
    Ranger. New York: A.S. Barnes, 1976.

Sandoux, Jean Jacques. Racism in Western Film from D.W. Griffith
    to John Ford: Indians and Blacks. New York: Revisionist Press,
    1980.

Sarf, Wayne Michael. God Bless You, Buffalo Bill: A Layman's
    Guide to History and the Western Film. East Brunswick, NJ:
    Associated University Press, 1983.

Solomon, Stanley J. Beyond Formulas: American Film Genres. New
    York: Harcourt, Brace & Jovanovich, 1976.

Weiss, Ken, and Ed Goodgold. To Be Continued.... New York:
    Crown Publishers, 1972.

Wright, Will. Six Guns and Society: A Structural Study of the
    Western. Berkeley: University of California Press, 1975.

NAME INDEX

* = Indian actor playing an Indian;
+ = non-Indian actor playing an Indian

TOPICAL INDEX

(with associated images and themes in parentheses)

BAD INDIANS (bloodthirsty, vengeful, threat to progress)

BAD INDIANS (cont.)

    562, 570, 579, 590, 620, 636, 653, 689, 702, 713, 714, 778, 794,
    797, 807
raping 265, 459, 620, 636, 725, 730
spying 228, 692
torturing whites 3, 42, 54, 330, 656, 661, 687
using fire (burning at the stake, flaming arrows) 27, 40, 48, 87,
    156, 158, 168, 171, 213, 279, 287, 364, 400, 411a, 475, 481,
    552, 574

BAD WHITES (Indian as victim)

crooked politicians, businessmen or outlaws after Indian land or miner-
    als 30, 87, 114, 214, 221, 272, 283, 294, 309, 368, 376, 378, 400,
    407, 419, 439, 447, 463, 470, 471, 493, 508, 513, 516, 543, 551,
    567, 574, 575, 576, 584, 607, 638, 647, 648, 654, 667, 684, 703,
    711, 737, 767, 775
hanging or lynching 45, 569, 636, 759
Indian agent 58, 195, 205, 214, 354, 355, 388, 390, 398, 400, 416,
    523, 551, 667, 698
Indian-hating hero or main character 212, 330, 482, 513, 523, 544,
    560, 570, 602, 606, 628, 648, 656, 675, 728, 737, 748
jailing 35, 39, 577
pushing Indians off their land 22, 69, 421, 651
raping or seducing 110, 137, 155, 253, 434, 546, 551, 612, 663, 674,
    697, 710, 711, 721, 725, 753
revenge 31, 79, 84, 146, 602, 748
tricking or rejecting friendly Indian 83, 501, 535
unjustified attack 58, 564, 600, 737, 738, 792
villain inciting Indians to war 31, 155, 224, 231, 249, 250, 252, 262,
    269, 273, 281, 282, 295, 297, 311, 315, 322, 325, 338, 340, 342,
    345, 354, 356, 360, 368, 372, 375, 380, 385, 386, 389, 396, 401,
    402, 417, 422, 423, 440, 447, 453, 457, 462, 470, 471, 485, 491,
    496, 508, 509, 513, 516, 518, 522, 527, 528, 538, 541, 555, 556,
    562, 563, 565, 567, 568, 592, 603, 631, 648, 658, 683, 684, 696,
    707

COMMENTS OF FILM CRITICS ON INDIVIDUAL FILMS

acting 15, 16, 25, 41, 43, 62, 85, 99, 113, 124, 132, 141, 154, 158,
    186, 229, 246, 271, 272, 288, 293, 308, 340, 355, 382, 408, 410,
    414, 422, 433, 446, 462, 480, 506, 527, 530, 532, 534, 565, 570,
    577, 586, 602, 606, 624, 640, 682, 687, 698, 727, 773, 777, 780,
    786, 787, 789
authenticity 1, 16, 26, 52, 66, 78, 90, 111, 113, 134, 197, 219, 226,
    246
comic portrayals 54, 209, 275, 374, 662, 689, 734
common plot and stereotypic formulas 33, 34, 68, 107, 145, 175, 184,

COMMENTS OF FILM CRITICS ON INDIVIDUAL FILMS (cont.)

GOLD AND OIL (cont.)

    493, 503, 513, 538, 546, 571, 607, 647, 648, 657, 722, 731,
    824
oil 150, 151, 241, 373, 375, 611, 684

GOOD INDIANS (noble savage)

adopting of a white man 107, 157, 200, 234, 242, 278, 304, 310,
    474, 482, 521, 606, 648, 698, 738, 739, 771, 790
adopting of white woman 175, 240
college football player or pro athlete 5, 96, 159, 227, 443, 820,
    822
doctor 355
female friend or companion to a white 97, 240, 278, 534, 590, 600
female rescuer of white man 1, 3, 4, 19, 24, 29, 40, 97, 118, 180,
    297, 304, 512, 600, 656, 671, 731
female rescuer of white woman 3, 23, 24, 37, 72, 97, 131, 154, 172,
    297
friendly, wise, peace-loving leader (often contrasted with a hostile
    leader in the same film) 219, 329, 394, 414, 439, 472, 487,
    492, 511, 512, 513, 523, 525, 528, 532, 552, 556, 565, 585,
    586, 592, 618, 650, 683, 688, 727, 738, 787
half-breed female 604
half-breed male 119, 149, 400, 569, 621, 673, 724, 746, 763, 767,
    776, 793
helping hero stop a crime, uprising or villain 234, 399, 418, 462,
    468, 512, 525, 527, 577, 628, 647, 659, 729, 749, 782
male friend, companion or guide to a white 12, 96, 141, 149, 161,
    182, 211, 219, 266, 285, 304, 305, 310, 314, 322, 323, 326,
    328, 359, 370, 379, 380, 382, 404, 408, 420, 424, 447, 462,
    472, 487, 495, 497, 501, 511, 512, 525, 528, 532, 540, 562,
    577, 579, 595, 607, 615, 624, 633, 647, 651, 658, 662, 670,
    678, 684, 690, 691, 692, 704, 709, 715, 726, 736, 740, 749,
    760, 761, 763, 765, 772, 780, 782, 786, 788, 794, 795, 796,
    800, 803
male rescuer of white man 158, 200, 202, 227, 268, 446, 504, 651
male rescuer of white woman 21, 33, 57, 83, 108, 144, 163, 173,
    193, 211, 446, 595, 673
performer in Wild West Show 103, 209, 272, 785, 813
policeman 200, 235, 809
Pony Express rider 263, 341
rodeo performer 272, 662, 716, 761
serving as U.S. soldier 203, 204, 227, 421, 473, 531, 532, 613,
    619, 629, 633, 719, 734, 747, 755, 757

GOOD WHITES (paternalism)

adopting a female Indian 42, 81, 627

GOOD WHITES (cont.)

female friend and protector of Indians   205, 275, 413, 569, 650,
    728, 743
female rescuing Indian   11
Indian agent   137, 368, 419, 426, 573, 728
male friend and protector of Indians   239, 253, 257, 278, 353, 378,
    398, 407, 495, 584, 592, 607, 615, 650, 651
male rescuing Indian woman   23, 199, 232, 653, 661, 721
male rescuing Indians from villains   148, 168, 179, 191, 196, 283,
    371, 390, 425, 457, 463, 574, 583, 592, 607, 647, 790
male stopping hostility   253, 349, 470, 471, 485, 490, 491, 496, 505,
    507, 508, 513, 516, 526, 528, 538, 556, 565, 568, 573, 575,
    593, 608, 615, 624, 638, 648, 658

HISTORICAL EVENTS

Black Hawk War   66
Chisholm Trail   393
Fetterman & Wagon Box Massacres   454
French & Indian War   230
Iwo Jima   633
Lewis & Clark Expedition   534
Little Big Horn, Battle of   18, 74, 214, 217, 348, 445, 464, 609, 667,
    693, 738, 818
March of the Cheyenne   651
Sand Creek Massacre   581, 743
Sioux Outbreak of '68   205
Washita Massacre   738

HISTORICAL FIGURES--INDIAN

Attla, George Jr.   820
Black Hawk   66
Brant, Joseph   181
Chato   745, 753
Cochise   349, 388, 414, 439, 487, 525, 592, 677
Crazy Horse   531, 532, 667, 796, 800
Geronimo   68, 318, 325, 349, 414, 422, 439, 444, 470, 475, 506, 573,
    623, 638, 808
Hayes, Ira   633
Hikatoo   181
Ishi   803
Joseph, Chief   779
Little Big Man   532
Mangas Coloradas   535, 592
Mills, Billy   822
Montezuma   107, 122
Parker, Quanah   526, 636
Pocahontas   10, 38, 176, 483

HISTORICAL FIGURES--INDIAN (cont.)

Osceola   501
Pontiac   230, 559
Powatan   10, 176, 483
Rain in the Face   214
Red Cloud   206, 235, 491, 587, 588
Sacajawea   534
Santana   144, 146, 147
Santanta   526, 527, 733
Sitting Bull   214, 226, 229, 275, 413, 490, 521, 523
Taza   525
Tecumseh   347, 462
Thorpe, Jim   443

HISTORICAL FIGURES--WHITE

Boone, Daniel   3, 177, 282
Bridger, Jim   784
Buffalo Bill   see   Cody, William
Carson, Kit   1, 34, 232, 266, 327
Clark, William   534
Clum, John   573
Cody, William (Buffalo Bill)   210, 213, 244, 248, 275, 287, 302, 335,
      358, 375, 785, 816
Cortez   122
Crockett, Davy   420, 533
Custer, George A.   18, 64, 74, 203, 214, 218, 281, 287, 348, 445,
      455, 464, 523, 609, 667, 693, 699, 738, 816
Davis, Jefferson   66
Earp, Wyatt   366
Grant, Ulysses S.   816
Hickok, Wild Bill   287, 304, 332, 683, 800, 816
Huston, Sam   115
Lewis, Meriwether   534
Lincoln, Abraham   66
Oakley, Annie   275, 413
Rolfe, John   38, 176
Scott, General Winfield   66
Serra, Junipero   546
Slaughter, Texas John   623
Smith, Captain John   10, 38, 483
Taylor, Zachary   66

HISTORICAL LOCATIONS (threat to progress)

Canadian Northwest   101, 123, 124, 134, 146, 152, 161, 264, 406
Chisholm Trail   393
Hudson Bay   173, 337
Jamestown   176
Los Angeles   676, 755

LAWMEN (threat to progress, friend to whites)

Canadian Royal Mounted Police   41, 202, 226, 264, 265, 329, 345,
     472, 490, 521, 625, 762
Texas Rangers (including the Lone Ranger)   289, 291, 305, 314,
     326, 562, 607, 623, 714, 816

LITERARY SOURCES

Arnold, Elliot, Blood Brother   414
Barrie, James M., Peter Pan   190, 498
Bell, Zachary, Joe Panther   787
Berger, Thomas, Little Big Man   738
Bloom, Harold J., "The Yellow Tomahawk"   528
Borland, Hal, When the Legends Die   761
Callahan, Robert, Daughter of the West   400
Cody, William, The Great West That Was   213, 244, 248
Coleman, Caryl, "Black Gold"   373
Cooper, James Fenimore   51, 82, 144, 185, 235, 260, 285, 338, 352,
     377, 424, 497, 579, 637, 797, 802
     Deerslayer   82, 352, 579, 802
     The Last of the Mohicans   51, 144, 260, 285, 377, 637, 797
     The Pathfinder   497
     The Pioneers   338
     The Prairie   381
Cottrel, H.D., and Morosco, Oliver, "Half Breed: A Tale of Indian
     Country" (play)   160
Craven, Margaret, I Heard the Owl Call My Name   769
Freuchen, Peter   265
Gessner, Robert, Massacre   272
Grey, Zane   135, 204, 283
     Desert Gold   135, 283
     The Vanishing American   205
Harte, Bret
     "The Half Breed"   110
     "The Outcasts of Poker Flat"   296
Hill, Ruth Beebe, Hanta Yo   828
Huffaker, Claire, Nobody Loves a Drunken Indian   734
Huston, James, An Eskimo Saga   777
Jackson, Helen Hunt, Ramona   39, 112, 233, 288
King, Charles, Warrior Gap, A Story of the Sioux Outbreak of '68
     206
Kopit, Arthur, "Indians" (play)   785
Lafarge, Oliver, Laughing Boy   271
Lawton, Harry, Willie Boy, A Desert Manhunt   728
Le May, Alan, The Unforgiven   627
London, Jack, "The Story of Jees Uck"   165
Longfellow, W.W., "Song of Hiawatha"   15, 85
May, Karl   647, 658, 670, 678, 684, 690, 703, 709
Michener, James, Centennial   801

LITERARY SOURCES (cont.)

Momaday, Scott, House Made of Dawn   755
Olson, Theodore, Arrow in the Sun   743
Parker, Gilbert, The Translation of a Savage   142, 276
Quinn, Theodora Kroebek, Ishi in Two Worlds   803
Roberts, Kenneth, Northwest Passage   330
"Rose of the Rancho" (play)   94
Royle, Edwin M., "The Squaw Man" (play)   95, 132, 255
Sandoz, Mari, Cheyenne Autumn   650
Scarborough, George, "The Heart of Wetona" (play)   137
Serling, Rod, Requiem for a Heavyweight   639
Slaughter, Frank, The Warrior   583
"Strongheart" (play)   96
Twain, Mark, The Adventures of Tom Sawyer   127, 247, 308
Wellman, Paul I., Apache   506
Yorgason, Blaine, Windwalker   815

LOVE AND MARRIAGE: INDIANS AND WHITES

half-breed male and Indian female--death or rejection   11
half-breed male and Indian female--happy ending   120, 131, 824
half-breed male and white female--death or rejection   116, 119, 147,
      160, 510, 536, 582, 823
half-breed male and white female--happy ending   110, 569, 680
half-breed male and female   159, 256
half-breed female and white male--death or rejection   108, 330, 365,
      384, 397
half-breed female and white male--happy ending   123, 124, 125, 128,
      142, 165, 183, 544, 597, 648
Indian male and half-breed female--happy ending   398, 400, 420,
      592
Indian male and half-breed female--rejection   411a
Indian male and Indian female--death or rejection   36, 39, 65, 70, 77,
      88, 202, 233, 271, 272, 288, 406, 484, 618, 644, 650, 728, 757,
      815, 828
Indian male and Indian female--happy ending   15, 17, 22, 25, 42,
      43, 52, 59, 78, 85, 86, 103, 112, 197, 200, 259, 272, 355,
      394, 469, 506, 577, 625, 638, 644, 815
Indian male and white female--death or rejection   5, 21, 63, 96, 109,
      157, 193, 203, 205, 227, 240, 285, 421, 443, 551, 570, 591,
      675, 679, 687, 715, 716, 734, 755, 761, 763
Indian male and white female--happy ending   30, 99, 130, 143, 341,
      526, 822
white male and Indian female--death or rejection of the Indian   8,
      14, 29, 32, 42, 52, 61, 62, 71, 79, 95, 103, 104, 132, 196,
      201, 202, 204, 238, 255, 271, 358, 385, 395, 414, 437, 461,
      466, 474, 480, 482, 489, 534, 538, 546, 561, 570, 573, 584,
      585, 589, 612, 663, 716, 722, 738, 739, 756, 757, 777, 805
white male and Indian female--happy ending   19, 46, 118, 122, 129,

LOVE AND MARRIAGE: INDIANS AND WHITES (cont.)

137, 151, 170, 191, 194, 257, 276, 277, 321, 483, 497, 510,
522, 560, 565, 588, 603, 618, 664, 689, 717, 725, 732, 735

SERIALS

serials 92, 126, 156, 162, 171, 177, 178, 185, 192, 213, 223, 244,
248, 252, 258, 260, 264, 266, 278, 279, 281, 286, 297, 301,
302, 303, 304, 305, 314, 315, 316, 317, 322, 323, 335, 341,
344, 345, 351, 357, 367, 369, 417, 428, 475, 516, 555, 566

STUDIOS AND DISTRIBUTORS

Aaron Spelling 742
Affiliated Dist. 151
Allied Artists 490, 507, 547, 576, 583, 584, 597, 608, 649, 664,
688, 710
American 66, 68, 79, 158, 159, 165, 530, 654, 655, 673
American Inter. 711, 786
Arrow 167, 178, 179
Artcraft 121, 140
Artists' Creation 787
Associated Artists 387
Assoc. Exhibitors 209
Associated First National Pics. 160, 169, 173, 175
Associated Producers 144, 634
Astor 410
AVCO-Embassy 743, 804
Aywon 154, 172
B.C.R. Productions 197
Biograph (Amer. Mutoscope) 1, 2, 5, 8, 11, 12, 14, 16, 17, 22,
24, 37, 39, 42, 43, 50, 59, 72, 74, 76, 80, 88, 96
Bison 34, 40, 45, 52, 58, 62, 64, 65, 69, 75, 78, 84, 91, 102
Bluebird 113, 119, 130
Box Office Attraction 100
Buena Vista 533, 593, 606, 609, 623, 646, 685, 700, 720, 727, 735,
771, 822, 829
Burrough-Tarzan 292
Canadian 226, 762, 805
CBC 806
CFDC 810
Champion 27, 30
Charles Davis Prod. 237
Chevron 740
Cinemacolor 81
Cinerama 693, 714
Clark Cornelius Corp. 161

STUDIOS AND DISTRIBUTORS (cont.)

William Fox Vampire Productions   109
W.S. Hart   133
Wolper   779, 828
World   20, 118

TRAITS OF INDIANS (bloodthirsty and noble savage, conflict be-
    tween Indian and white culture)

college education (female)   118, 120, 241, 358, 398, 407
college education (male)   5, 47, 63, 78, 88, 91, 95, 109, 111, 130,
    147, 157, 159, 160, 187, 188, 193, 200, 203, 207, 227, 241,
    272, 355, 400, 421, 443, 511, 530, 680, 781, 786
drinking (drunken Indian)   47, 53, 91, 172, 330, 366, 416, 511,
    538, 633, 668, 734, 757, 768, 810, 822
generosity   84, 622, 643
gratitude   3, 20, 23, 24, 37, 57, 72, 148, 159, 172, 179, 187, 278,
    447, 448, 504, 566
honor   45, 50, 77, 100, 119, 447, 467, 501, 562, 720
loyalty and friendship   40, 45, 193, 443; see also GOOD INDIANS
respect for courage   17, 533, 665, 688, 756
vengeance or justice   7, 12, 18, 37, 40, 50, 55, 56, 65, 79, 87, 93,
    101, 103, 113, 137, 146, 155, 160, 163, 164, 167, 189, 208,
    215, 219, 248, 303, 362, 433, 434, 448, 452, 454, 458, 459,
    466, 467, 496, 506, 528, 546, 569, 581, 586, 600, 654, 672,
    674, 675, 679, 682, 687, 694, 696, 697, 705, 709, 711, 712,
    715, 718, 723, 725, 731, 737, 741, 742, 746, 753, 756, 786,
    792, 826

TRIBES

Abenaki   330
Apache   68, 75, 78, 133, 138, 167, 195, 303, 312, 324, 349, 350,
    388, 394, 412, 414, 422, 427, 438, 439, 449, 457, 458, 468,
    470, 475, 481, 482, 487, 488, 492, 496, 502, 506, 515, 517,
    525, 529, 530, 535, 536, 541, 547, 549, 551, 561, 571, 573,
    577, 580, 586, 590, 591, 592, 599, 600, 617, 623, 626, 634,
    635, 638, 646, 647, 648, 649, 651, 656, 657, 658, 660, 669,
    670, 672, 675, 677, 678, 684, 688, 690, 695, 698, 703, 707,
    708, 709, 714, 715, 722, 731, 733, 737, 745, 747, 748, 753,
    760, 763, 808
Arapahoe   219, 575, 692
Arikara   643
Aztec   107, 122, 376
Blackfoot   137, 224, 232, 319, 437, 490, 596, 792, 814
Cherokee   310, 407
Cheyenne   25, 26, 184, 217, 224, 440, 478, 552, 559, 564, 581, 588,
    650, 683, 687, 723, 729, 743, 794, 815

196   The American Indian in Film

TRIBES (cont.)

Chumash 653
Cliff Dwellers 107
Comanche 189, 289, 297, 369, 487, 526, 556, 561, 570, 601, 605,
    620, 631, 643, 645, 646, 660, 671, 689, 703, 709, 765
Creek 222
Crow 756, 784, 815, 824
Delaware 144, 352, 606
Fox and Sauk 66, 443
Hopi 78, 700
Hoppe 79
Huron 70, 82, 144, 352, 377, 579, 762, 797, 802
Inca 126
Iroquois 36, 117, 313, 424
Kiowa 22, 433, 526, 544, 620, 627, 682, 704, 712, 763
Mayan 644
Modoc 512, 610, 632, 784
Mohawk 37, 181, 565
Mohican 51, 57, 70, 82, 117, 144, 165, 260, 285, 352, 377, 424,
    579, 797, 802
Navajo 204, 221, 241, 267, 271, 357, 362, 400, 434, 447, 452, 485,
    551, 654, 684, 691, 701, 716, 720, 758, 775, 826
Nez Percé 139, 685, 727, 779
Northern Cree 472, 521, 736
Ojibway 15, 85, 246, 469
Osage 467, 611
Oseka 425
Ottawa 459
Paiute 387, 602, 728, 783, 784
Papago 134, 742
Pawnee 507, 585, 593, 706, 738
Pima 633
Pueblo 76, 241
Seminole 441, 501, 527, 545, 553, 680, 694, 710, 787
Seneca 181
Shawnee 347
Shoshone 327, 421, 534, 608, 628, 678, 739, 784, 794
Sioux 14, 15, 16, 17, 29, 56, 64, 65, 71, 85, 103, 162, 184, 198,
    200, 206, 214, 216, 217, 218, 224, 226, 228, 229, 235, 242,
    272, 281, 336, 440, 445, 454, 455, 464, 467, 490, 491, 493,
    509, 521, 537, 538, 540, 552, 557, 587, 589, 593, 594, 595,
    609, 618, 630, 641, 662, 666, 667, 668, 686, 693, 700, 702,
    705, 713, 739, 757, 759, 768, 785, 801, 804, 822, 824, 827
Siwash 191
Ute 95, 450, 513, 761
Yahi 803
Yaqui 61, 88, 113, 135, 211, 322, 504, 563, 576, 661, 681, 724
Yuma 75